Praise for But Whe

Shannon's story is riveting, and at times, overwhelming. She tells her story with strength and courage. I don't doubt that many victims will find Shannon's story important in their own journey of healing. Shannon is leaving an important legacy with her book.

— DR. JAMES SHIELDS, DOCTOR OF
PSYCHOLOGY AND SPECIALIST IN CHILD
SEXUAL ABUSE TREATMENT

Very powerful! Shannon does such a good job of putting memories and feelings into words, as well as describing the conflict within herself between good and bad memories.

— RETIRED DISTRICT COURT JUDGE JOHN
LAUN, CHAIRMAN OF THE SEXUAL REVIEW
BOARD FOR THE ARCHDIOCESE OF
LOUISVILLE

The past twenty years have produced scores of articles and news headlines about the reality of child abuse and the sins of clergy who have violated their vocation and call to serve Christ and His Church by such horrendous acts. Few accounts, however, provide such a thorough witness to the reality of what a victim-survivor endures and the great challenges of the path of healing that must follow.

— MOST REVEREND JOSEPH E. KURTZ,
ARCHBISHOP EMERITUS OF LOUISVILLE

I am proud to have represented The 243. Those brave souls willing to take a public stand against one of the wealthiest and richest institutions in the world, The Catholic Church. Their courage forced The Church to take financial and public accountability and to offer pastoral and other counseling for anyone abused by the hands of clergy or other employees. It forced The Church to make policy changes to deal with allegations of abuse differently and to believe victims who were abused. And chief among those leading the charge for change and reform was Shannon Shaughnessy Age. May we all persevere to overcome our pain and channel it for positive change the way she did.

— HANS G. POPPE, ATTORNEY FOR THE 243

Shannon has written a book for survivors of clergy sexual abuse, but also for all survivors of any abuse/injury and for all who seek to grasp Jesus' hand as He pulls us from the darkness to His own wonderful light. Her work is a blessing for all of us who are members of the Body of Christ.

— MARY ANGELA SHAUGHNESSY, SCN, J.D., PH.D., SENIOR DISTINGUISHED FELLOW OF CATHOLIC EDUCATION, LOYOLA MARYMOUNT UNIVERSITY, LOS ANGELES, CALIFORNIA

If you seek TRUTH ... read this. If you want to experience COURAGE ... read this. If you ever feel lost and need inspiration to KEEP ON GOING ... read this. Join Shannon in her journey from VICTIM ... to SURVIVOR ... to THRIVER!

— CRAIG HERINK, LMFT, TRAUMA THERAPIST AND ABUSE SURVIVOR

But When I Fly

A JOURNEY OUT OF DARKNESS

SHANNON SHAUGHNESSY AGE

Lynn,

Thank you for your support!

Blessings,

Shannon

KEL-CON
PUBLICATIONS

This book is dedicated to my husband, Steve, who has been my rock for over forty years, to our sons, Austin and Patrick Age, who were in the eye of the storm for so long, and to all the people who told me I needed to write this down for the world to see.

It is, of course, also dedicated to my Sissy, Debbie Shaughnessy Ernspiker, who never came out from under those horrible years.

Furthermore, it is dedicated to the wonderful woman who finally gave me the courage to do this. Thank you, Dr. Mary Angela Shaughnessy, a Sister of Charity of Nazareth, known to me as my friend Angie. I will be forever grateful for your encouragement and help.

Table of Contents

Foreword

MARY ANGELA SHAUGHNESSY, SCN, JD, PHD

When I first met Shannon Shaughnessy Age (we are not related), she had been referred to me by a mutual acquaintance because I am an attorney who represents sex abuse victims. Shannon and I "hit it off" immediately. In the ensuing weeks, I met her husband, Deacon Steve.

In her book, *But When I Fly: A Journey out of Darkness*, Shannon shows the reader that it is possible to cast the darkness aside and learn to fly, even if one is stricken by sin, injustice, tears, and pain. First, a person must acknowledge the darkness that is there before one can fly out of it, rather than seek some pseudo-rescue in its shadows. Far too few of us, whatever our woundedness, dare to take the necessary steps out of the darkness. Shannon does this in a way both remarkable and blessed. Like David before Goliath, she confronts the ugliness of sex abuse in the Catholic Church, and both shines and becomes the light of truth. There is no greater journey, struggle, or victory.

My small contribution to this wonderful woman and her story is to have encouraged her to continue to tell it, both orally and in writing, while she fights for justice for victims of clergy sex abuse. Shannon is, like St. John the Baptist, a prophet pointing the way toward Jesus who is the Way, the Truth, and the Light. Shannon shows us that there is no way to

Jesus except through the muck, and that there is no muck so bad that Jesus cannot pull us through it to salvation.

Shannon has written a book for survivors of clergy sexual abuse but also for all survivors of any abuse/injury and for all who seek to grasp Jesus's hand as He pulls us from darkness to His own wonderful light. Shannon's is a story that must be told, for all who suffer from sex abuse and from any other pain. Her work is a blessing for all of us who are members of the Body of Christ. Indeed, as the hymn promises, "I will raise you up, I will raise you up, I will raise you up on the last day."

I am blessed and humbled to call Shannon Shaughnessy Age my friend and to recommend this book to you, the reader.

Mary Angela Shaughnessy, SCN, JD, PhD
Senior Distinguished Fellow of Catholic Education
Loyola Marymount University
Los Angeles, California

But Why?

The question I ask myself most often, as have many, is why have I written this book?

What is the purpose?
What good will it do?
Does it matter?

They are all good and valid questions. After working on this book for years, I continue to grapple with what these answers are.

I guess the real reason is, so the story of this little girl doesn't die one night with an old woman. The child who endured so much needs to be heard, to be believed, to be honored for her endurance, her resilience, and her strength that got her through not only the abuse, but also all the years of PTSD, anxiety, panic attacks, and dissociative episodes. My decision to write this book wasn't an easy one but a must.

As you dive in, I invite you on my journey, one I kept silent for years. It's a vulnerable one, a tough one to read for many, but it's a story of hope. And it's hope that I want you to embrace.

This is not a book about Catholic bashing; it is about learning from past mistakes. I am a faithful cradle Catholic. It is not against priests; some of my dearest friends are priests. It is not in outrage against Catholic clergy; my own husband is a deacon. Knowing this, I hope you will be able to read my story through the lens that I've been able to live it—as someone who has seen the underbelly of the church and has come to the other side still deep in faith, in love with my God, and an active member in the Catholic Church. Use this as a point of reference in areas throughout my story that perhaps may be challenging to understand.

This book does, however, address the way abuse was handled by the Church before the lawsuits of the early 2000s. Looking back and digging deep into the allegations of decades, it is sometimes hard to understand how this scandal was allowed to happen and go on for so long. But we must view those years and those responses through the lens of *that* time and era to understand it. We know more about the psychology of an abuser now. We are aware that an abuser doesn't get over those tendencies. We can't send them to a rehab and expect them to be safe with children and not engage in abuse again. *That* was the professional opinion and mindset then. We know better now.

Let this be your guide. In fact, let *me* be your guide. If you have not endured abuse, my hope is that this will be of help. If you have survived abuse, you will find you are not alone.

Perhaps, too, my experience will someday be used in a meaningful way to prevent others from enduring what I have. I hope that seminaries and universities use my story as a tool to teach about the spiritual damage done when a member of the clergy sexually abuses children. No child should ever have to endure any type of abuse, but sexual abuse by a clergy member—which is tied into the very sacraments the Church holds so dear—damages the very spirit and soul of the most innocent. It is only because of the grace of God and the prayers of so many that I am today a faithful Catholic and the wife of an ordained permanent deacon of the Roman Catholic Church.

I am living proof of how a master pedophile grooms not only the victims but also the family of the victims. Fr. Kevin's path wasn't just the typical path of so many priests who were moved from parish to parish. He was moved to six different states, as well as being stationed in South Korea. Fr. Kevin and my parents wrote many letters to each other during the years the abuse was happening. Some of these letters are referred to in the story. You will also see pictures taken by him of us, and of him with us, taken by our parents.

This has not been easy to write, and it will not be easy to read. *Please* read it anyway. Read it for Little Shannon and Little Debbie, who were four and six when their abuse started. Read it for all the others who have lived through abuse. Read it for those who, like my Sissy, lived through the abuse but never outran it.

Never forget, however, that hope is within reach. Hope, because since 2002, when all the lawsuits first started coming out, we have seen real change in the response of our Catholic Church. In June 2002, the United States Conference of Catholic Bishops adopted the Dallas Charter for the Protection of Children and Young People. I am proud of the changes, especially here in my own Archdiocese of Louisville. In Kentucky, we have also changed laws protecting children against childhood sexual abuse.

Every time I see change, I feel like I'm adding a feather to a set of wings I didn't know I needed to fly. Because, you see, I had flown before.

I remember the first time I flew—in an airplane, on the swing set, from my dad's arms. That type of flying is fun and many times breathtaking. But it is different from the kind of flying in my story. This flying requires my own set of wings, and every time I share my story, those wings are strengthened. There is freedom in flying. And in hope, forgiveness, and peace. This story is about *that* kind of flying. And it's also about how we can let others fly too.

So, come sit with me awhile. Go on a pilgrimage with me. It's not a journey for the faint of heart, but what quest worth taking is?

Blessings,
Shannon

I am broken.

Let me say it again. I. Am. Broken.

They tore me apart. Sexual abuse. Alcoholism. Emotional neglect. Emotional abuse. But ...

My God is greater than what happened to me. He is greater than any of their actions or non-actions.

And yet, why have I been able to live through it when my Sissy and so many others couldn't and haven't? That is the question that always haunts me. I know I am not better in any way than those who haven't been able to move through it. The other side isn't visible to them. Sissy and I were raised by the same parents, had the same abuser, had the same circumstances growing up. But our lives were much different. She is no longer here. Why am I still standing?

My sister believed in God. She went to church. She believed in Jesus. She believed she was saved. And she was consumed by the darkness of our past in the end. I can only pray that she is resting in the arms of our Savior as I write this now. Just rest, sweet Sissy.

Darkness always lurks. Sometimes I can't run from it, but I haven't stopped trying. When I feel the nightmares calling, when God's "man" starts singing his lies to little girls (to me), when the stories I want to hide from still find me, I am reminded that abuse isn't something you cure. It's something you endure. I am enduring.

Shannon, undated

One

My family—my father, mother, and older sister—was a typical family of the time. Dad was the breadwinner. He worked for the Kentucky Air National Guard. My mom was a happy little stay-at-home wife. My sister and I were typical small kids who played and got into little tiffs.

In the summer when the ice cream truck would come around, Mom would send us out to get a treat. Because Debbie was the oldest by twenty-one months, she was given a nickel and a dime to pay for us both. Debbie would tell me I could have the bigger coin, and she, being the kind, big sister, would take the smaller one. After a few times of me coming back crying with no ice cream and a nickel in my hand and Debbie smiling with her ice cream, Mom figured out what Debbie was doing. From then on, Mom made sure to give Debbie two dimes for the ice cream truck.

My parents were cradle Catholics who both went through twelve years of Catholic school education. In addition, my dad's parents were both 100 percent Irish Catholic. My grandfather came to America at eighteen in 1908. My grandmother was the first child born to Irish immigrants. Dad's maternal uncle was a priest. My maternal grandmother scrubbed floors at a Catholic church during the Great Depression so her six kids could attend school there.

As with most families, there's the family the world sees and then there's the reality.

Dad was an alcoholic from his early twenties. He once told me that while stationed in England in the early 1950s, after a drinking binge on hard liquor, he landed in the hospital. He told me the doctor had warned him that one more binge like that and his liver would be gone, and he would die. Instead of quitting, Dad switched to drinking beer only, and in his fifties, he again switched to wine. Alcohol was always a part of Dad's life.

My mother drank occasionally; her drink of choice was gin bucks. She didn't drink beer at all, joking that she must have Baptist eyes because beer gave her a headache! She very rarely, and only in later years, complained about Dad's drinking. It was only after he died that she would ever use the word alcoholic to describe my father. To her, drinking only beer didn't qualify as a legitimate alcoholic.

My father was very short and had *the* large "Shaughnessy" nose. He told us that, while his family was loving towards him, he was the butt of many jokes and a favorite of bullies.

At seventeen, he accidentally shot himself in the arm while cleaning a gun. In the new age of antibiotics of the 1940's, he was given massive doses of penicillin to keep from losing his arm. It did save his arm, but as a side effect, he lost all his hair, and it never came back. The bullying increased exponentially.

When my parents met in 1957, my father had lost his driver's license because of his drinking, and therefore didn't own a car. My mother drove them everywhere they went.

My parents married seven months after meeting. They didn't have the money for a honeymoon, so they went to stay with my dad's uncle, the priest at a parish in rural Kentucky. They spent the week in the rectory with Fr. John. Mom got up each morning and made breakfast for her new husband and his uncle, the priest.

I don't know when Dad got his license back, but he was definitely driving again by the time my sister was born in 1958, because Mom said Dad had to come home from work and take her to the hospital to give birth to Debbie.

THE EARLY YEARS OF THEIR MARRIAGE WERE TYPICAL OF THE TIME.

Our little family seemed very stable and happy. Our parents loved both of their children and doted on them accordingly. Dad's brothers, sisters, nieces, and nephews adored him. He was the life of the party wherever we were, but when we got home, Debbie and I became pros at walking on eggshells.

Mom was very happy to be a stay-at-home wife and mother. In the early years, meals were on the table when Daddy came home. While not the best housekeeper, Mom was a wonderful cook. When Debbie started first grade and I was four, I remember standing on a chair at the stove as Mom taught me how to make chili. I always sat next to her at church, leaning against her. She sewed a lot in those early years—clothes for Debbie and me, as well as tiny outfits for our Barbie dolls.

Every evening on his way home from work, Dad stopped at his favorite liquor store and hung out with his fellow drinking buddies and drank a few beers, before bringing home his carton of eight Sterling beers. This also was the place he would often bring me when he would run out of beer. He would sit me up on a stack of beer cases in the stock room with some Cheetos and Orange Crush as he talked and joked with his buddies.

My parents' Catholicism was obviously central to our family dynamic. It was the ruler by which our behavior was measured.

In 1964, our little family moved to a new home across the street from property where a new Catholic church was to be built. My parents became part of a group of founding members for that church. The church was a part of our DNA, and even the electric extension cords used in building the rectory were plugged into our house. The church first met in the basement of the new rectory, and then in 1965, the new church itself was opened. It was the center of our lives and everything we did.

In 1964, my father became friends with the chaplain where he worked. This priest's name was Fr. Kevin Cole. He, too, was an alcoholic, so over their favorite beers, they became fast friends. As Dad didn't have any friends he brought home regularly, Fr. Kevin checked all the boxes.

Fr. Kevin soon became a frequent visitor to our home. At first, he would be there for dinner, and as time went on, he became a part of our family. He was included in every part of our lives, whether it be through church, family meals, picnics in the park, or even weekend getaways or vacations. After Debbie and I went to bed at night, Fr. Kevin, Mom, and Dad would have long conversations, most often about theology or the goings-on at the Air Guard. Always, Dad's Sterling and Fr. Kevin's Stroh's beer bottles could be heard clinking on the table as they drank.

Dad was thrilled to have his new friend and so was Mom. And Fr. Kevin met my parents where they were in their life and belief system and made *them* feel safe. He was a priest. He was Irish. And he was Catholic. In my parents' eyes, you couldn't get any safer than that!

Unless you are a pedophile.

Sweet Daddy, where did things go so wrong?

You were my hero, yet you brought the devil home in your weakness. I adored you, but I feared you, as we walked on eggshells. I now understand that is typical in families that have alcoholism as a part of their dynamics. Your disease made you the life of the party, for sure. But unfortunately, it tore our family to shreds.

You were, I now understand, what is referred to as a highly functional alcoholic.

You never missed work.
You were a leader and stand-up member of your church and community. You were beloved to your extended family as well.
You were extravagant in your help of others, even though you had little yourself.
You welcomed so many lost souls to our dinner table.

I have followed you in rule following, even knowing that all those stupid rules you made us live by never kept us safe. It drives Steve and the boys crazy. Thank God neither Debbie nor I ever found any happiness or help in the bottle.

Daddy, I will be forever confused by how I feel about you. I love you so much, more than I can explain. I miss you so much. And I am so damn mad at you for what all happened to us. (I am sorry; I had to say it.)

I tried to go to Al-Anon meetings about twenty years ago with a dear high school friend, but the people and stories scared and triggered me. Maybe someday I will give it another try,

Daddy, I forgive you. I just want to run to you and have you give me your warm hug I remember so well. I need you so much, Daddy! I need to know you love me, despite everything that happened so many decades ago.

Shannon, 2022

Two

It first started when Fr. Kevin asked if he could say our bedtime prayers with us and tuck us in. It seemed like a small enough thing that a good priest would do, right? This man of the cloth would lead these children in prayer. No problem.

"Sure, Father. Thank you for helping while Dottie does the dishes after dinner, and I'll get us another beer."

"Okay, so how about I give you a rest tonight, Dottie? Let me see to the girls' baths! You and old Bern go relax in the living room, and I'll have them ready for bed in no time at all!"

This was a typical conversation between Fr. Kevin and my parents.

As a child of the 1960s, this didn't seem abnormal to my parents, and as a four-year-old child, I didn't know any better. Of course, looking through the lens of today, I realize everything about this situation was wrong. And a different decision by my parents at this point could have changed everything.

Everything.

In what is now known as typical grooming, Fr. Kevin usually brought Debbie and me small gifts that any four- and six-year-old would adore.

Little doll babies or candy usually were the norm. He would let us "ride his foot" as he bounced us up and down with squeals of delight in front of our parents. He would tickle us until we were screaming for him to stop. Our parents were so happy that they had this wonderful priest who didn't mind the antics of little children. And, of course, Fr. Kevin was happy too. His plan was working.

FR. KEVIN WAS UNUSUAL FOR THE TIMES IN THAT HE WAS NOT ASSIGNED TO A CHURCH, AS WERE MOST PRIESTS.

Because he was a professor of theology, he lived in an apartment on the campus of a local Catholic college with other priests who also taught there. He would occasionally fill in at mass at different parishes when it was needed. Through Dad, he was introduced to our pastor, and became a sub when needed. And so, his next step was to offer to babysit for Debbie and me at sleepovers at his apartment at the college.

"Bernie, just think, you and Dottie could have a night out and not have to worry about those little cuties waking you up early in the morning. You could actually sleep in!"

And so, the sleep overs began. Only, they were weird. We never got to sleep in bed with our parents, but now, we slept in bed *with* Fr. Kevin because there was only one bed. Not to worry, he's a priest!

Soon after that, Fr. Kevin was going on weekend trips to the lake with us. He always kept the time lively by supplying plenty of alcohol for my dad and quick wit with my mom. He tried to teach my mom how to swim. My mother, who never touched water except in a shower due to a childhood swimming accident, soon was floating in a lake with Fr. Kevin's enthusiastic tutoring.

In the summer of 1967, summer camp for the Air Guard was to be in Savannah, Georgia. Fr. Kevin had a grand plan he offered to my parents.

"Bernie, you fly Dottie and the girls down and we'll have a vacation together. We can get adjoining rooms, and I'll take care of the girls in my room, so you can have a week with Dottie. It will be like a second honeymoon for you, but you can still see the girls during the day!"

During that week, we swam in the pool and in the ocean with Fr. Kevin as my parents lounged in chairs. I can remember riding to different places with trees on both sides of the road dripping with Spanish moss. The trees seemed to completely cover the road, to the point it seemed you were driving through a dark tunnel.

We slept in *that* room with Fr. Kevin the whole week while our parents were in an adjoining room. Our parents felt we were so safe, so they enjoyed the nights with each other.

IN 1968, THE PUEBLO CRISIS HAPPENED, WHERE THE NORTH KOREANS CAPTURED AN AMERICAN VESSEL.

My dad's guard unit was called up for active duty. For the next eighteen months, my dad was, for the most part, gone. He was stationed at an Air Force base in Missouri and then on to Japan in 1969. Because of his teaching duties, Fr. Kevin was kept home much more than Dad, but he did end up being sent to South Korea in the fall of 1968.

While Dad was gone and Fr. Kevin was still at home, he made sure he was there to help Mom out whenever he could. He was happy to take us on "dates," giving Mom a break.

In 1969, Dad and Fr. Kevin came home for good, and life went back to what we considered normal. Fr. Kevin was again around all the time, but his drinking appeared to be even worse.

To Dad, drinking was an outlet.

To Fr. Kevin, it was his courage, perhaps to do things that were theologically wrong and evil.

Dad could no longer keep up with him.

In 1970 when I was ten and Debbie was almost twelve, she talked to her best friend about what was going on with Fr. Kevin. Like the telephone game, her friend told her mother. The mother informed her that it was not right, and she suggested Debbie tell her mom. Debbie followed that advice. Mom told Dad, but Dad didn't believe her.

Six months later, I innocently told Dad about one of our tickle games at Fr. Kevin's apartment. This game was not something any adult should be playing with a child, though I thought it was normal.

We had been playing it for years, longer than I could remember. My dad's face got very red, and he left the room. He and Mom talked for what seemed like hours about who knows what. Dad didn't talk to us.

After it had been quite some time since we saw him last, Dad told us we were going to see Fr. Kevin. He was by this time a pastor in a local parish. For some reason, he was no longer at the Air Guard working with Dad. I now question if my dad had something to do with Fr. Kevin's abrupt departure from the Guard, but I guess I will never know. I have no idea why Dad felt we needed to see Fr. Kevin again. Dad told us when we saw him, we couldn't hug Fr. Kevin or sit on his lap during the visit.

Fr. Kevin sat behind a desk.
I don't remember anything that was said.
I just remember being so very confused.
I never saw Fr. Kevin again.

I am so deeply blessed. I have a wonderful, loving husband, two sons that will be there for me if I need them, and grandchildren that I adore. I have friends of over fifty years, as well as new friends. I have a faith community that has held me in their hearts and arms and raised me up when I couldn't raise myself up. Yes, I am truly blessed.

And yet, today my heart hurts. I ache for my first family, the one that nearly destroyed each other.

Eighteen years ago today, Mom passed away.
Dad's been gone for over thirty-two years, and Sissy for three and a half years.

In my mind, Little Shannon peers into the window of my childhood home, watching her family. Today, she wants to remember the good days, the fun, tender memories.

Sitting on Daddy's lap.
Mom sewing Barbie doll clothes.
Riding bikes with Sissy.
Shutting out the bad things.
Only good things today.

I will hold onto those memories today and think of my first family with love and tenderness, because on those days, I was indeed blessed.

Shannon, January 6, 2019

Three

As a teenager and young adult, I knew something was *wrong* with me.

I feared all sorts of things that nobody else I knew was afraid of. Certain sounds and smells brought a feeling of pure terror. Specific songs made me panic uncontrollably. As I was starting to be interested in boys, I was terribly scared of them, though I couldn't for the life of me figure out why.

In my freshman year of high school, I coordinated and taught a preschool religious education program at our church. I adored working with these five-year-old kiddos. They touched my heart. I also was coaching our church's seventh and eighth grade cheerleading squad. As a cheerleader myself, I loved the sport and sharing it with others who did too.

In an early year of high school, a nun—who I only recall as Sister Rita—became our pastoral associate at church. She helped me with the planning and curriculum for the preschool religion program. She was a very gentle and kind soul. My father, seeing that I admired Sister Rita, suggested that she might be willing to take me to a convent to show me how nuns lived. He seemed to think life in a convent would be a good choice for me. Possibly he thought that the lifestyle of a nun would allow us to not be triggered by our past trauma.

And so, I went for an overnight visit to the convent. I was shown to a very small room in which I was to stay that night. It had a twin bed, a chair, a sink and a very small closet.

As I looked at the room, I could not imagine that this could be *all* I wanted in life. I wanted something different.

I wanted a family and children. The nuns were all gracious and wonderful, but their lifestyle was not what I envisioned for me. I didn't feel that calling.

But I wasn't sure what my calling was.

I was a teenage girl, who like my father, was ignored because I wasn't deemed as attractive as the other girls my age. And, if I'm being honest, I didn't blame them. When I looked in the mirror, I saw an unattractive girl. I saw a girl who was brutally shy, unable to speak her thoughts and didn't have enough confidence to say anything anyway.

But I loved God. I loved children. And I was interested in boys in my class. However, I was also terrified of them for no reason I could come up with. Thank goodness, those boys weren't interested in me, because there was no telling what could have happened to this fragile girl had I been handled in the wrong way at that impressionable age. God knew I had already endured too much.

DEPRESSION STARTED SHOWING ITS UGLY FACE.

In what I believe was my father's ill-designed attempt to protect us from boys who might hurt us, he began to tell Debbie and me that we were ugly, stupid and unlovable. That no man would ever want us. Basically, that we were worthless. And, the even sadder part was we both believed it wholeheartedly. I believed I would live my life alone and lonely. For in addition to my dad's words, I also knew that, while I craved the love of a man, intimacy terrified me. I was at a loss as to why, but it did nonetheless.

> I hoped and prayed I would just go to sleep one night and never wake up. I prayed for it diligently. Life was unbearable.

My father had so many strict rules that prevented us from having a normal life. We both were constantly grounded for the smallest infraction. Grounded meant no phone, no television, no newspaper and no contact with friends other than at school. The "sentence" was usually anywhere from a week to six weeks. Our friends were very seldom allowed to come to our home. He taunted my sister and me constantly about our lack of boyfriends. We both came to believe our lives were useless.

I began to take small amounts of my mom's prescription medicine and hide it. I was trying to come up with enough pills to commit suicide. By my senior year in high school, I thought I knew which ones might do the trick, but repeatedly, my attempts would fail as I would wake up in the morning—alive—and even more depressed than before. I was a failure even at suicide.

LOOKING BACK, I REALIZE I WASN'T A FAILURE AT EVERYTHING.

I wasn't the best student, but I was probably above average academically. I wasn't popular, but I wasn't alone. I had a few friends at school who I am still close to today and who probably saved me from myself. Maybe I could have had more friends, but I have been told by some that it was very hard to get to know me (And quite frankly, I've heard that my whole life.). I thought if they really knew me, they wouldn't stay.

In retrospect, I *was* complicated. I didn't understand myself or what was going on to even be able to share with someone. So, I didn't. I kept it in, hoping I could hide from the parts of me that just. didn't. make. sense.

Like my irrational fear of someone being under my bed. I was in high school, a time when most had outgrown a fear like that, and yet I began having horrible nightmares that someone would reach out from under the bed and grab me. I would wake my mom up with my screams. I was so convinced someone was there that Mom would have to get a flashlight, get on her hands and knees on the floor with me, and confirm no one was there. After I finally calmed down, I would get back in bed, being very careful that I didn't let my arms or legs hang off any part. To this day, this is still a fear I face.

Not all nightmares happen while asleep. In fact, I began to realize that what I daydreamed about most turned into a most terrifying nightmare. Men.

I graduated high school in 1978 and became increasingly depressed, having moved from seeing my friends at school every day to seeing them very rarely as our paths diverged. I was frustrated with my first job. That year, at a family Christmas party, a cousin suggested that I apply to a school to become an X-ray tech. I had no clue what that even was. But with her help, I was accepted into a tuition-free school at a Catholic hospital in July 1979.

Academically, I excelled in this program, but yet again, I didn't fit in. The other students in my class had steady boyfriends and were out having a good time in life. Because I was still living at home with all the rules and alcohol-induced rages of my father, I was reluctant to engage in true friendships with the four other girls who made up our class. I only dated now and then but never was asked out for a second date. And that was okay because they scared me to death. I didn't quite understand why though.

In June of 1981, I met the man who would become my husband and I immediately knew I had found the one. While I was still terrified of men, for once I thought I might have a chance for a life with a family of my own with a man who didn't terrify me. In 1981, I graduated from X-ray school, passed my national boards, took my first job in a hospital as a tech, and fell madly in love with Steve.

We were engaged on Christmas Eve. For my Christmas present, I got an engagement ring. But he got a young woman who blew hot and cold.

One minute, I was happy and in love; the next, I was crying on the floor and talking in the voice of a six-year-old.

One minute, he would hold my hand and try to kiss me; the next, there was that crying six-year-old again.

One minute, I was fine; the next, I was suddenly afraid of everything again. Certain songs, the smell of beer, the tickling were absolute terrors.

One minute I was a joyful young woman about to start this wonderful chapter of her life, and the next minute I was sure I was just going to die.

OUR MINDS HAVE A WAY OF PROTECTING US, EVEN WHEN WE DON'T ASK THEM TO.

I had no idea I was navigating two ends of a spectrum of emotions. I didn't know that things would trigger me. And in fact, it wasn't until years later when I would be triggered again, that Steve would remind me this had been a pattern while we were dating. I was terrified of relationships, but he wasn't terrified of me. He loved me for me, even if I didn't know who that was.

A few months before our wedding, I asked my dad to see if he could find Fr. Kevin so that he could be the priest to preside and witness our love for each at our wedding. Dad told me, with tears in his eyes, that he didn't know how to find Fr. Kevin. It was years before I understood those tears.

In October 1982, Steve and I were married and became the family I always wanted. Thank God, Steve stuck with me. He took the vows of in good times and in bad, in sickness and in health to heart. He loved me when I could allow it and gave me space when I needed it. But most importantly, he stayed. He stayed through both of our confusion and pain. He stayed when I had no idea why I was like I was. He stayed when I was twenty-two and when I was six.

He. Just. Stayed.

Never ending; it's always there.
The darkness.
The shadows from the past.
The love songs that he sang to me.
"Strangers in the Night." "Blue Spanish Eyes."
Extra dry martinis. Stroh's beer. Cigarette smoke.
And uh. And uh. And uh.

Going on special dates in the dresses Mommy would make for us. Spaghetti and meatballs for me; ravioli for him. I was only recently able to eat my first ravioli at fifty-nine years old.

Him screaming as he entered the kitchen of a restaurant because his food wasn't cooked to his liking.

Him laughing at Sissy in the ocean because he felt the water get warm while he was holding her.

Him telling Mommy not to let us have beans for dinner before we would spend the night with him because we would stink up the bed when he "tickled" us.

I still have trouble driving after dark, perhaps due to always being the one who had to sit next to him in the car. That was the "hot seat." He liked to get a few feels in during the car rides; perhaps that, as well as the liquor he always had on board, caused the multiple auto accidents we were in with him driving.

Shannon, 2019

Four

In October 1985, we had our first son, and for the first time in my life I understood a love that could cause me to protect it with my own life. This tiny little baby was so loved by us—by me! He brought a joy into my life that I had never imagined possible. He was perfect in every way, as every mother's child is supposed to be.

Just four months after Austin's birth, and three months after Debbie's first child was born, my father was diagnosed with stage 4 colon cancer. The "C" word ran rampant in our family on both sides. Dad had seen his mother and sister die early, awful deaths from the disease. He was determined that if he received a cancer diagnosis, he wouldn't ask for any treatment.

That is, until he fell in love with his first two grandchildren, the only two he ever met. Treatment wasn't a nice-to-have; it was a must. He loved those babies, and every day with them mattered. His goal was to see both of those babies turn one. And he did. Two weeks after my niece's first birthday, we lost Daddy.

And I was lost after Daddy's death.
I was his favorite.

Even though most parents wouldn't admit it, my parents did. Mom and Dad had each chosen a favorite child around the last year that Fr. Kevin was around. Debbie was Mom's, and I was Dad's.

Dad was terribly hard on Debbie all the time. She had a very sensitive and tender heart, and she would cry at the drop of a hat. Dad used that to torment her to tears and then relentlessly ridicule her for the tears he had caused her to cry.

Watching the way Dad treated Debbie taught me a lesson. You. Don't. Ever. Cry. And so, I became the *strong* one.

I wouldn't even blink, no matter what the next punishment was. I just took it. Dad admired this in me, he later told me, and I became his favorite because of it. He thought I was tough. And that made him proud.

Not to be left out, Mom became Debbie's solace. They had always been close. While Dad was gone from 1968–1969 on deployment with the Guard, they spent many nights in Debbie's bedroom having "big girl" talks, to which I was not included. I would sit with my back to the outside of Debbie's door and beg to be let in, but they told me I was too young to understand.

Now, with what Debbie was going through with Dad, Mom was ever present to comfort her but not for me. I asked Mom many years later why she had never comforted me. She told me she hadn't thought I needed it because I was so *strong*. While she never said anything to Dad about his behavior in front of us, Mom was always there to pick up the pieces but only for Debbie.

THEIR TREATMENT OF US CAUSED GREAT JEALOUSY BETWEEN DEBBIE AND ME.

After Daddy died, I once asked Mom why she consoled Debbie but never defended us from Dad's wrath. She told me she thought it would have caused him to explode. But oh, what I would have given (and taken) to see her defend us!

With Dad gone, Mom and Debbie leaned on each other. But just as when I had leaned on Debbie's bedroom door so many years before, I was not allowed in. In a rare conversation about this with Mom, she shared that Dad had voiced his concern and worry that I would be alone after he died while Debbie would have her for support. And to an extent, Dad was right.

But what they both didn't count on was Steve and Austin. My little family led me through the early stages of grief. And my grief was very complicated.

I mourned a man who I had great fun within our silly teasing games.

I mourned as the child of a parent who favored me, but who had also made me feel worthless and unlovable.

I mourned a man whose alcoholism had caused many financial burdens that we as a family had had to endure.

I mourned a man who had allowed my sister and me to believe that each other was the enemy.

And so, the gap between my mom and sister and I grew. I tried not to let it bother me. But of course, it did.

STEVE AND AUSTIN BECAME MY FOCUS IN LIFE. WE BECAME THE FAMILY I WISHED I HAD HAD AS A CHILD.

Austin was one of those babies any mother would wish for. He was a joy. He was always happy. As long as he had a clean diaper and a full tummy, he was truly an easy baby. Perhaps because his first year had been shared with the illness and death of my father, he took pity on his poor parents and just thrived. He wound our hearts and marriage with his love. His little hugs healed the brokenhearted child in me.

Mom and Dad had been able to soak up Austin's joyful nature for the first four months until Dad became sick, watching him at their home when I was at work. At that time, my sister stepped in to help. She was a stay-at-home mom with her daughter and appreciated some extra income. And Austin got to spend quality time with his cousin. They played, giggled, and rolled through that time as a brother and sister would. They adored each other and were each other's first friend.

I'm grateful that friendship blossomed because it allowed me to rekindle mine with my sister.

In 1988, Debbie had her second child. I was the first person, other than the doctor and hospital personnel, to hold him. Although his big sister wanted her mom to take him back because she wanted a sister, the rest of us were in love with this bundle of fire!

The next year, we welcomed our second son, Patrick. We fell in love again! Though full term, he was a tiny little guy, so little that one of his first outfits was the shirt from an Alvin the Chipmunk stuffed animal. The staff called him Peanut. Austin loved the title Big Brother, but most of all, he just wanted to know when that baby would stop crying! (What I didn't know is that the answer would be fourteen months.)

Patrick was a fast learner. He rolled over for the first time before he was six weeks old! He was a momma's boy. He didn't like for me to be out of his sight—ever! He was happy so long as I was either holding him or within his range of sight. And he adored his big brother, and as soon as he started scooting, he tried to follow him everywhere.

WE FELT OUR FAMILY WAS COMPLETE. LIFE WAS AS GOOD AS I KNEW GOOD COULD BE. IT WAS BETTER THAN ANYTHING I HAD EVER HAD.

I started a new job in the fall of 1991.

While Mom and I had never had a very deep relationship, we were speaking.

Debbie and I spent more time together so the kids could too.

My relationships with two of the most important women in my life were about as good as they would ever be. But we were just so different in every way.

Different became something I became used to because I realized ... *I* was different.

Today is one of those days.

So very hard. I dread this day every year. I know it will come, and it will pack a punch like no other. It rams me in the gut and pierces my heart. It leaves me bleeding, crying, and mourning.

Today is Mommy's birthday.
And today is Fr. Kevin's birthday. He was born on the exact same day and year.

Just one year, I would love to be able to forget that.

I would love to be able to just be a little girl who celebrates her mommy's birthday.

Or even a fifty-eight-year-old grandmother who celebrates her deceased mother's birthday.

But there are these sneaky little details that make that impossible.

Details like my grandmother telling my mommy that it wasn't right that Fr. Kevin bought Sissy and me new underwear every time he brought us home from an overnight visit.

Or Grandma telling my mommy that a priest shouldn't be wanting to give little girls baths or taking pictures of it. And Mommy defending Fr. Kevin. Every. Time.

Or Mommy and Daddy writing letters to Fr. Kevin about wanting him to keep us in his hotel room on vacation so they could have some alone time together. Which meant Sissy and I had alone time together with the rapist/pedophile.

I forgive you, Mom, I do, but I just haven't been able to forget. And I haven't been able to separate your birthday from his. I don't know if I will ever be able to do that. For those years, we all celebrated them together. And now, it's just so tangled up and knotted together. And so, I am filled with anguish, mourning, and hell on March 18 every year.

I hope you can celebrate the day of your earthly birth well today in heaven.

I love you, Mom.

Shannon, March 18, 2019

Five

Part of a caterpillar's transformation requires it to live within a cocoon. Like a warm hug, it is pivotal for it to become a butterfly. I didn't realize that my friends would be my cocoon.

THE FRIENDS WHO STEVE AND I MADE AT OUR FIRST CHURCH AS A MARRIED COUPLE CHANGED OUR LIFE IN WAYS WE NEVER COULD HAVE FORESEEN.

As a young married couple with two small children, we became involved just as my parents had when I was a youngster. The church became our hub, and while that made sense to this cradle Catholic, Steve was beginning to build his faith. Catholicism wasn't yet a part of his DNA.

Steve and I started doing mission work in Appalachia in a group we helped to start called Sow the Word. Our little world revolved around our church and a small group of friends who did mission work with us. There were probably ten-to-twelve families in this core group, and when we weren't planning a mission trip or on one, you would likely find some—if not all—of us hanging out or having dinner together. Our children, many of whom were about the same age, became fast friends.

Families aren't always bound by blood; we were living proof of that. Our families were totally enmeshed with each other.

Our friend group had a common denominator in our faith and core moral values. We saw our world through that lens. We wanted to raise our children to share that faith and to always believe in giving to other people. And our children gave the adults a very different perspective in life. While adults saw overwhelming poverty in the mission field of Appalachia, our kids saw other children who liked to play with puppies and kittens just like them. Our children taught us much about who the "other" might be.

I didn't know it yet, but I would one day need help myself. At one point, I would become an "other."

I thank God that he allowed us to go to Appalachia and build these strong friendships before the missing pieces of my life's puzzle were found. You don't know until you know. I didn't know, then. But once I did, I realized I could never not know. The faith that grew for both Steve and me and our friendships are what sustained us through the first years of my healing journey after I uncovered my past. While we have been gone from that parish for years, many of those friendships remain. God does indeed supply all our needs.

FRIENDS HAVE BEEN THE GLUE, BESIDES STEVE AND THE BOYS, WHO HAVE HELD ME TOGETHER.

Some of my friends from grade school and high school, though as varied as the colors of the rainbow, have pulled me up by the bootstraps more times than I could count. They have listened to me in my despair, anger, grief, and happiness. They celebrate every step forward that I can take but never lose hope in me when I falter and backslide.

These are the friends who saw me through the storm. These are the ones who walked beside the "me" I call ghost girl because I have parts of my life I will never remember. That girl that some days might speak to you, but other days would barely speak at all, because she had lost her words. My friends spoke anyway. These friends lent a sense of normalcy to a world so out of control. They didn't know it at the time, but they saved my life in the time they spent with me and the things we did together.

And for them I will be forever grateful!

You can't wait until life isn't hard anymore to decide to be happy.

I was watching a video on social media and a young woman dying of cancer made that statement. It hit me right in the heart. So many days, I am so stuck in the past that I forget I have TODAY. I have a chance each day to do something good, something fun, something happy. Today is the next chance out of all those bad days and years. And I must not hope that tomorrow may be better ... a good day ... a happy day ... because I just can't be happy today. As Sissy found out, sometimes we don't get a tomorrow.

And so, I must learn to treat every day as the treasure it is, a gift of opportunity. I must open it eagerly every morning, perhaps even with a smile on my face, thinking of what joys might lie in this new day to come. Just what might I discover in my garden today or in meeting a friend today or in a walk with Steve or in snuggles with my grandchildren? What adventure might I find in a new book I am reading? What solace might I bring to a friend who's sick? Where will God take me on this journey today?

And if there is suffering in my soul, I will be happy that I have lived another day to feel it, for many have not. And I will hold my Sissy close to me in my heart.

Shannon, June 2021

Six

In the fall of 1991, after years of searching, Steve decided he wanted to join the Catholic Church. We had been working in the mission group for almost two years, and this work and the people who worked with us had drawn Steve in. Over the next three months, we planned his baptism and confirmation to welcome him into his faith family. Of course, Steve couldn't complete these sacraments at our home church; he had to do it in the mountains where his faith had blossomed.

Because he wanted to be baptized where he felt he had received his call, thirty-two people traveled to a small chapel in the mountains of Appalachia to welcome him into the church on February 8, 1992. Though his parents held no love for the Catholic Church, they did make the trip to witness it, which meant the world to Steve. My mother came along too, and she was overjoyed. It was a wonderful and glorious day! I felt that our little family was right where we belonged. Our marriage was strong, our children were healthy, we both had good jobs, and we had a nice place to live. We now shared the same faith.

WHEN I DIDN'T HAVE NIGHTMARES, THIS WAS THE
LIFE I WOULD DREAM ABOUT.

During the months leading up to Steve's baptism, a feeling of unease
returned. I once again started having a sense that something was wrong,
but I didn't know what. I was again scared and startled by certain
sounds, songs, and smells. Driving in the dark terrified me.

> I felt like there was something in my memory that was trying to
> get out, and that it was horrible. I tried my best to ignore it all,
> but it kept happening.

On May 7, 1992, I was talking on the phone with my mom, and she
shared that one of my cousins was in the hospital undergoing treatment
for alcoholism. I was shocked because this cousin was always so
completely in control of her life (or so I thought). Mom then explained
that her father had sexually abused her when she was a child. I didn't
know what to say.

Then, she said, "You do know that Fr. Kevin abused your sister, don't
you?"

My heart felt like it had fallen out of my chest. I could barely breathe.
Suddenly, a wall broke. Hell's doors opened. The devil jumped out and
named himself.

And I knew.

The memories flooded into me. The terror coursed through my veins. I
wanted to scream and cry and die. Every part of me hurt. The smells of
beer and cigarettes and sex. Him singing love songs to me as he raped my
tiny little body. The horrible things he made us do.

I was four.
Debbie was six.

It took me three days to tell Steve. It had taken him almost ten years to decide to join the church, and three months later, I wanted to run screaming away from it. How do you tell someone you have been married to for almost a decade that something this horrible happened—and you hadn't remembered it?

You just do.
His response was one I never could have expected.
He said he *knew*.

I wasn't the first one to tell him. Daddy had asked him on the day of our wedding to be gentle with me because a priest had messed with me when I was a very little girl. Daddy knew. Steve knew. I was stumbling through this new revelation.

My husband, who knew from my own father that I wasn't the virgin bride I thought I was, had always referred to me as such. I asked him, tears rolling down my face, why he had done that? His response was that I was a virgin to him when we married because I had had no choice back then.

And now the tears in Daddy's eyes when I asked him to find Fr. Kevin to preside at our wedding made sense.

Little girl lost, where do you go?

Hiding under a desk or on the curtain's pleats or just somewhere deep in your long-ago mind?

Will you ever stop running, searching for a safe place to be?
Will you ever find comfort, arms that are soft that will hold you free from harm?

Is there a place without all those awful sounds and smells and pains waiting for you somewhere?
Is there a place you can go to sleep and not awaken with terror in your eyes and a scream in your throat?

Now I lay me down to sleep. Please God, if you can't make it stop, please just take me!

Shannon, 2018

Seven

I had to start over. Where should I go for help?

Some may turn to their parents. Others to their siblings. Those weren't options for me. But my faith was. I didn't feel comfortable going to my pastor because he was a priest, so I contacted the deacon at our church who happened to be Steve's godfather. I told him my story and that I didn't know what to do. My mental status was all over the place. I couldn't function in my daily life. I asked for his help.

Instead of being the support I was looking for, he asked me why, if it hadn't bothered me so much in all the preceding years, wouldn't it just be better to forget about it? I was shocked. Was he suggesting that I just bury it?

A week later, the phone rang. It was him, and while I was very apprehensive to talk to him because I had felt judged as to the worthiness of my need, I listened anyway. He begged for my forgiveness and offered to help me to get therapy in place. He contacted the order of priests to which Fr. Kevin had belonged and found that he had died the previous year. While I was relieved to know that I would never have to face Fr. Kevin again, I felt cheated out of the justice of letting him know the impact of what he had done.

The deacon shared my story with the vicar, the head of the order of the priests, and a meeting at the deacon's home was scheduled so he could talk to me in person and see what could be done to support me.

When I arrived for the meeting, I was grateful to find that the vicar wore street clothes; no remnants of the priest he was were displayed. I thanked him for that, knowing it could have triggered me that day.

He told me they were aware of Fr. Kevin and his history of pedophilia. He shared that the order would find me a therapist and cover the cost. The vicar seemed sincere in his grief over what Fr. Kevin had done to Debbie and me. He also agreed to meet with Debbie if and when she should decide she wanted help, which she did a few months later.

In 1992 at the age of thirty-two, I began therapy with my first therapist. Her office was on a church campus, and she was a former nun whose brother was the current auxiliary bishop in our archdiocese. Martha started teaching me the coping skills I still turn to today when memories flood back.

FIND A SAFE PLACE.

If you can't be in the safe place you have created in your home, then you must be able to do it in your mind.

If you see me out, even today, with my eyes closed, seemingly in a trance-like state, you can know that, in my mind, I am throwing my beach towel on the sand. Smoothing out every fold. Putting on my sunscreen and my sunglasses. Laying back and opening my book. Here, I won't let him touch me. This is my safe place.

In December of that year, during a particularly brutal session, Martha suggested I try to picture myself getting rid of all the memories without having to look at them again. Perhaps, she suggested, it would be like throwing those memories back at Fr. Kevin and letting him deal with them. Just try to imagine that I was vomiting all that sick stuff out of me and on to him. Throw up on Fr. Kevin's face in the toilet.

I vomited for three days.
I also became six years old again.

I broke down at work, sitting on the floor, rocking, and crying. Steve came to pick me up. He brought me home, and as I now call it, I stayed little for three days.

I continued therapy with Martha for years, going once or twice a week. It was brutal. Every time I thought I was making progress; a new memory would knock me down on the floor. I was in a major depression for years. As I told Martha, I felt there was no use in trying to get up and out of the depression. I knew that something was always going to throw me back there again. And so, I settled into the muck of my depression. I understood the muck. I had been in and out of it for more than half my life.

During this time, my family was affected as well. The boys were so young and didn't understand that mommies are supposed to be happy. They had a mommy who was clinically depressed. They had a mommy who loved them so much but who was in so much pain she could barely navigate everyday getting by.

Steve never knew who he was coming home to: the adult, the rocking six-year-old who could barely talk, or the broken one who yelled and cried out her agony. I unintentionally hurt them deeply, and I don't know if they will ever be able to forgive me or if I will ever be able to forgive myself for those years of disruption I caused in all our lives. I hope someday they will understand that I am so very sorry. I was just trying to stay alive.

During these years, Mom shared with me that Dad had never told her why he suddenly decided to end our relationship with Fr. Kevin. He never shared with her my story about Fr. Kevin's tickle game. Debbie finally told her after she started her therapy that Fr. Kevin had abused both of us and that I was his favorite in every way.

While I was in therapy, Debbie started hers but became mad. ALL. THE. TIME. She yelled at me. She yelled at Mom. She yelled at her husband. She yelled at her kids. She, too, was clinically depressed. More than anything, I remember her rage at what had been done to us.

DEBBIE HAD FOUND HER VOICE, BUT I HAD LOST MINE.

Anger was a scary thing to me. Fr. Kevin and Dad had both many times been very angry and screamed at us when they were drunk. I remember many scenes where one or both would embarrass me with their behavior in public.

Anger was an emotion I refused to address in therapy because I wasn't ever allowed to feel it. Martha wanted me to scream out my anger during sessions. Hit pillows. Get it out! But I couldn't. I had taught myself to not react so that I wouldn't get Dad's wrath, which he poured out on Debbie when she cried. I couldn't now convince that little girl it was safe to let her anger out, even on a pillow.

Another fear that raised its head was being afraid of driving at night— which evolved into driving at all. Even during the day, I would look over at another car and see Fr. Kevin's face staring back at me. It took a while, but I finally shared my fear with Debbie. She told me we had been in at least three auto accidents with Fr. Kevin while he was drunk and driving us home. I then remembered a drive home where he ran into the back of another car, and my mouth hit the dashboard. He got out his handkerchief to stop the bleeding from my busted mouth. Then, he got out of the car and cussed the other driver out.

He was wearing his clerical collar.

His order later took away his driver's license at one point because of his many drunk driving accidents, but they didn't do anything about his pedophilia. In his later years, he took to riding buses everywhere he wanted to go, wherever that was.

Some days, I know it should be a "good" day. Nothing is going on to make it "not good." And yet, I feel such anguish and physical pain deep in my chest.

I feel as if my heart is breaking.
I can feel the despair of the little child I was.
She is still searching for help, for love, for rescue.

My attempts to console her leave the adult me sorrowful, lonely, and empty. I try to hold her, to rock her, to console her, but the depth of her pain is unfathomable. I feel the terror in her eyes: it is the same terror I feel every day of my life.

How, then, can I ever console that little girl when I haven't been able to console the adult?

Shannon, 2020

Eight

Sometimes you have a plan. Other times, God does. And His plan always wins.

In February 1995, a priest from Atlanta, Georgia, came to our church to do a three-day mission. When we got to church that Sunday, a dear friend told me his message might be hard for me to hear. I pondered on that and waited for his homily to start. He spoke about forgiveness and that we should forgive everyone of everything and anything.

At this point, I was starting to work on forgiveness in therapy but had not gone all in because it was hard to do. How do you forgive someone who deliberately and methodically did what Fr. Kevin had?

I hadn't figured that out yet. It was a hard pill to swallow. Fr. Kevin had died one year before the major portion of my abuse memories had flooded back, so I felt it was so unfair that he didn't have to answer for anything nor apologize for what he had done to us. And now this priest, who couldn't possibly understand what I had been through, was standing up on the altar demanding that I forgive everybody of everything they had ever done to me. I don't think so, buster!

And then *this* Fr. Bob paused. He said he knew that sometimes forgiveness can seem like too much to ask. He said he knew that forgiveness seems an unfair price for some sins committed. And he said he truly understood that to the core of his being, because he had been sexually abused as a child. It had caused horrible damage. And to make it even worse, his abuser was a priest.

The floor fell out from under me. I couldn't catch my breath. I felt gut punched. I wanted to wail in agony.

Instead, I silently cried. Tears ran down my face throughout the rest of mass. How could this man overcome the abuse and then become a priest? How much strength would that take? And could he teach me how to forgive?

After mass, Steve and a dear friend walked with me to meet Fr. Bob. Steve told him my story as I stood and cried on my friend's shoulder. He listened lovingly, and he said much; however, I don't remember his words. I only remember his blessing.

Two days later, what should have been a typical five-minute confession turned into three hours with Fr. Bob. It was the first time I had been to confession in decades. This was a milestone, considering Fr. Kevin used confession in our abuse.

Fr. Bob and I remained in close contact over the next year, working on forgiveness. No part of this journey was easy. But, with his help, as well as the help of the Holy Spirit, I was finally able to let go.

PIECE BY PIECE. STEP BY STEP. DAY BY DAY.

The underlying thread of our forgiveness work was building up to the culminating celebration mass of healing through forgiveness. When we spoke, we would also work on planning this pivotal moment in my life.

On February 17, 1996, Fr. Bob flew in and he—along with my therapist, Martha, and our closest friends—joined me in support of having this important mass. We chose to have it at the church at Mount St. Francis, Indiana, where Fr. Kevin is buried.

Each reading I selected was purposeful. It became my basis for forgiveness. The following are the Scripture passages I chose:

You are the people of God. He loved you and chose you for his own. So then, you must clothe yourself with compassion, kindness, humility, gentleness, and patience. Be tolerant with one another and forgive one another whenever any of you has a complaint against someone else. You must forgive one another just as the Lord has forgiven you. And to all these qualities add love, which binds all things together in perfect unity. The peace that Christ gives is to guide you in the decisions you make; for it is this peace that God has called you together in one body. And be thankful. Christ's message in all its richness must live in your hearts. Teach and instruct one another with wisdom. Sing psalms, hymns, and sacred songs, sing to God with thanksgiving in your hearts. Everything you do or say, then, should be done in the name of the Lord Jesus Christ, as you give thanks through Him to God the Father. (Colossians 3:12-17)

* * *

Love must be completely sincere. Hate what is evil, hold on to what is good. Love one another warmly as Christian brothers and be eager to show respect for one another. Work hard and do not be lazy. Serve the Lord with a full heart of devotion. Let your hope keep you joyful, be patient in your trouble, and pray at all times. Share your belongings with your needy fellow Christians and open your homes to strangers.

Ask God to bless those who persecute you—yes, ask him to bless them, not to curse. Be happy with those who are happy, weep with those who weep. Have the same concern for everyone. Do not think of yourself as wise.

If someone has done wrong against you, do not repay him with wrong. Try to do what everyone considers to be good. Do everything possible on your part to live in peace with everybody. (Romans 12:9-19)

* * *

Gospel selection:

Then everyone went home, but Jesus went to the Mount of Olives. Early the next morning, He went back to the Temple. All the people gathered around Him, and He sat down and began to teach them. The teachers of the Law and the Pharisees brought in a woman who had been caught committing adultery, and they made her stand before them all. "Teacher," they said to Jesus, "this woman was caught in the very act of committing adultery. In our Law, Moses commanded that such a woman must be stoned to death. Now, what do you say?" They said this to trap Jesus, so they could accuse him. But He bent over and wrote on the ground with His finger. As they stood there asking Him questions, He straightened up and said to them, "Whichever one of you has committed no sin may throw the first stone at her." Then He bent over again and wrote on the ground. When they heard this, they all left, one by one, the older ones first. Jesus was left alone, with the woman still standing there. He stood up and said to her, "Where are they? Is there no one left to condemn you?" "No one, sir," she answered. "Well then,"

Jesus said, "I do not condemn you either. Go, but do not sin again." (John 8:1-11)

While the mass was an emotional one, I was also joyful because I had made it to this point. The work I had put in was showing dividends. I was proud of myself.

After mass was over, we all walked to Fr. Kevin's grave site to vocalize what I was forgiving. I had written down each of the things I felt Fr. Kevin, through his abuse, had taken from me. Each person in attendance read a piece of paper and placed it and a rose on Fr. Kevin's grave —a grave I had seen for the first time that day. We then said a prayer for Fr. Kevin and for the repose of his soul. We went back to the dining hall and ate a light meal prepared by the staff.

It was a soul lifting day. A load of pain rose up and off me with the forgiveness.

Oh, grace of God, I could not travel this road without you. When I remember how blessed I am for your forgiveness of my every sin, I know there is freedom in letting go.

There has never been a person born whom God doesn't love just as much as me. Fr. Kevin is one of God's children too. Our Heavenly Father yearns for Fr. Kevin's soul as much as he does mine. And through the grace of God, I hope Fr. Kevin is resting in heaven with God Almighty.

Shannon, 2022

Nine

Therapy comes in different shapes and sizes. Martha was a soother, someone who never really pushed me but more coaxed me to work at my speed. Maybe I needed that at first, but it was time for a push.

IN THE LATE 1990S, I SWITCHED TO A NEW THERAPIST, CRAIG.

He led me to new types of therapy that would hopefully bring some healing in areas I had not been able to address yet. We worked to ease anxiety in many areas of my life. I was still afraid most of the time about so many things.

Still afraid to get on an elevator of only men but terrified to take the stairs for fear of who might be lurking there. Afraid of those songs Fr. Kevin used to sing to me. The smell of beer made me sick to my stomach. Cigarette smokers brought severe anxiety. I have burned holes in my First Communion dress from him.

And, in general, I was afraid of men. Period.

I worked in a large hospital, so having men as patients was part of my job, which made this fear a problem. I had previously worked as a mammography tech, but when I started a new job in 1991 after being home with the kids for several years, I found myself working again with male patients. Having to position them for X-rays triggered me. While later I would pivot to working full-time in mammography again, for a number of years this was a challenge that caused me to think I should change professions, or I would lose my mind.

As I worked with Craig, we tried to set goals of how I could overcome fears so I could live a more engaged life. Being afraid of men—and so many other fears people couldn't understand—held me back. Sometimes I would feel like I was making progress, and then another hurdle would jump up.

"What are you telling yourself to make you so afraid?" Craig would sometimes ask me.

I didn't have to tell myself anything. I had been taught all too well as a child that every person and thing was to be feared!

But guilt was a new emotion I needed to tackle, and it came full force when my mom suddenly died after a heart attack in 2001. We had never been able to mend our relationship. She was never able to be the mother I needed, and I was never able to be the daughter she wanted. And that is precisely what I still grieve.

GRIEF ISN'T SOMETHING THAT IS CLOSED UP AND BURIED WITH A CASKET. IT POPS UP AT ITS OWN CHOOSING.

After Mom's death, Debbie and I had to clean out my parents' house to sell, and I found grief there. Mom and Dad had lived in that house for thirty-seven years, and they were children of the Great Depression. They had saved everything. We even found Mom's first checkbook from 1945! It took us months to go through it all, and one day while going through the boxes, I found something that would open all the wounds once more.

It was a box filled with letters and pictures and presents. All from Fr. Kevin. Whether Mom had truly forgotten they were in the attic all those years while Debbie and I were going through therapy, I will never know. I do know it brought me to a new, gut-wrenching agony.

In those letters and pictures and bribes—yes, I consider his presents to us bribes—I found tangible evidence of what had happened. Living proof. There was even 8mm film of all our family times with Fr. Kevin. It sickened me. It made me gasp with pain. It made me wonder how our parents had not known what was going on for years.

In these letters, Mom spoke of how her mother thought she should be concerned with a priest who gave little girls baths. My mom told my grandmother to get her mind out of the gutter; he's a priest, for God's sake.

Or my dad telling my mom that Fr. Kevin had agreed to us staying in his hotel room. Dad couldn't wait to show my mother all his love, and Fr. Kevin was kind enough to give them time together.

And then came the letter where Fr. Kevin, the pedophile, asked my mom to send girl's clothes to him in South Korea during his deployment. It seemed that he had come upon an opportunity to work with orphans at the Catholic run White Lily orphanage for 195 girls, ages infants to fifteen. He had found his new hunting grounds while he was overseas. I pray for those poor, lost little girls.

Other letters joked about him cutting back on alcohol ... from thirty-six beers to thirty-five beers a day.

He talked of us going on dates with him when he returned to Kentucky. He wanted us to wear our "special" dresses that he liked.

He sent a picture of his desktop in South Korea. It was covered with pictures. All little girls. Photos of Debbie and me were in the center of the pictures. Did he switch those pictures around every time he sent a different letter to another little girl? I will never know.

It's late, and I know I should go to sleep to keep fear at bay. Being overtired seems to be a real mental mistake for me. I know how quickly it can take me down.

I've been doing great for the last few months. People think I am "back to normal." Boy, I guess I'm a great actress—I even almost fooled myself.

Late at night, it all floods back. I now accept that this will always be my life. I must keep a smile on my face ... no tears, no fears, right? Bullshit! It just takes so much energy to keep up the act.

Sanity is such an elusive thing for me. It almost always seems just beyond my reach, even as everyone around me thinks everything is okay.

The mask is back on. I must fit in or be discovered again. Sometimes I feel like giving up. I'm so tired.

Shannon, 1995

Ten

For nearly a decade, therapy was a part of my life. Then, finding the box of letters and photos in the attic took my breath away. It made what I knew was real, real. And in 2002, the stories of clergy abuse that began coming out of Boston brought all of the hard work I had done to a standstill. It seemed as if every time the wounds would start healing, something would rip them open. I was again back in the nightmare and flashback zone. Every new story made it all seem like it was right there with me every moment of the day.

IN APRIL OF THAT YEAR, THE STORIES CAME CLOSER TO HOME—IN LOUISVILLE, KENTUCKY, WHERE I LIVED.

Back then, newspapers were a part of everyone's daily routine, and each day, a new story highlighting another victim was shared. And if you thought you could dodge the papers, it was plastered on the nightly news every evening. In case you looked forward to a nice ride home after work, guess again; it was on talk radio too. I couldn't hide from it. It kept finding me.

A month later, Debbie and I wondered if there were other victims of Fr. Kevin out there. Neither Mom nor Dad had ever really discussed whether Fr. Kevin had abused other girls. The only clues we had were that he, according to my mom, usually stopped being friends with families about the time their daughter's reached puberty, and Mom, for reasons she never shared with us, believed he had abused his nieces too.

It was time for us to reach out because we needed to know if there were others. We needed to know we weren't alone. And I knew others needed to know that too.

In May 2002, I called the archdiocese office to find out if anyone had reported Fr. Kevin. I was told yes. I felt like I couldn't breathe. I asked if it was my sister who had made that report, and he said no. He then told me, "You do know he's dead, don't you?"

I was struck by his total lack of compassion. I told him Fr. Kevin might be dead, but he would forever be alive in our memories. I told him I wanted it to be shared with the press that Fr. Kevin had abused us. He then informed me that Fr. Kevin "wasn't one of our priests," so I should contact his order instead.

I hung up feeling as if I had been run over by a Mack truck.

The following day, I called the office of Fr. Kevin's order. Because they had paid for therapy for years for both my sister and me, I knew they couldn't deny the abuse. I told them the same thing: We wanted them to state to the press what Fr. Kevin had done to us. We truly believed he had other victims out there, and we wanted them to know we were too. An appointment was set up at my therapist's office for the order's representative to meet with me.

On the day of the meeting, the vicar was very calm and professional. He proceeded to tell me that they were a very small order, and they could not afford a lawsuit. I told him we didn't want money, we just wanted them to acknowledge our abuse in the press and that Fr. Kevin was indeed a pedophile priest.

He said that would be very difficult, because it could cause great damage to their order. Did he not realize that Fr. Kevin's victims dealt with great damage? I was convinced there were many others, and I wanted them to have the courage to speak their truth and be believed. I gave him an ultimatum. They would have a week to report it to the media. If it wasn't reported by then, my sister and I would join the class action lawsuit that was being formed against the Archdiocese of Louisville, which was gaining new survivors with each passing day.

WE WAITED A WEEK, AND ON MAY 22, 2002, WE JOINED.

By that afternoon, I had to inform our twelve- and sixteen-year-old sons what was going to be on the news that night. It was one of the hardest things I had ever done. I knew our lives would never be the same, but I felt we were owed justice.

Soon after, three more victims of Fr. Kevin came forward. They had seen the reports and decided the truth about him needed to be told.

It's one thing to speak my truth. It's another thing to relive it as you try to "itemize" what was done. Our attorney met with each victim and required that we provide a detailed account of our abuse all those years ago. And he needed the down and dirty details.

Each case showed not only what Fr. Kevin did but also his path around the Archdiocese of Louisville. It showed who knew what he was doing. It showed when he was sent away for treatment during those years and many times afterwards.

The pressure of unpacking my past—again—totally broke me. During the night in early June, Steve tried to wake me up from a nightmare, but I was gone. In my place was the six-year-old child. He tried talking to me, but he couldn't get me back as he had been able to for over twenty years. I was too broken. He called my therapist who quickly met us at his office and called a hospital to have me admitted.

The diagnosis was a dissociative psychotic episode.

I remember being so terrified. I remember thinking I was bad. I remember thinking I would never be safe again.

IT TOOK FOUR DAYS AND A LOT OF THERAPY FOR ME TO FIND MY ADULT VOICE.

But now, my terror had reached new levels. The memories were constantly swirling in my head like a tornado. I could not turn them off. I was put on a slew of medicines: one for depression, one for psychosis, another to help me sleep. Later, even more medicines were added to keep me calm. I felt like a stranger in my own body.

Steve and the boys didn't know how to act around me. The boys didn't know what to make of their mom, who would all the sudden seem more like a small child than their mother.

While I was in the hospital, my current therapist decided I should start seeing a female one. He felt, rightly so, that I would never be able to discuss the details of the trauma with him while feeling safe. So, the week after my discharge, I started seeing my third therapist, Anne.

She was everything a terrified girl in a woman's body could have hoped for in a therapist. She was gentle, kind and calming. She gained my trust quickly. Little Shannon felt like she had found a mother figure. The woman felt like she might find a way out of this to become a whole person.

Our goal this time was to learn how to process what had happened so long ago without letting the terror take over. I needed to feel safe enough to work through the past without it breaking me. I needed to be heard, but I had to be able to tell the whole story without the agonizing pain of the child who lived through it.

I was off work for one month. My aunt called and asked if I wanted a change of scenery, a space to breathe. She invited me and the boys to Virginia to stay with her, where I was pampered and had plenty of space to sleep and learn to be calm. It was a quiet time for which I will forever be grateful.

I began—again—that summer to take my life back. I began to let Little Shannon talk to me and tell her story without trying to stuff it back down. It was hard work, the hardest work I had ever endured. But for me to get better, I knew I had to do it.

"Reporting Abuse," *Courier-Journal* from 9-29-2002

Thirty-two of the plaintiffs who granted interviews said they or their parents reported their abuse to a senior pastor, a nun, a parochial school teacher or principal, or to the archdiocese – either when the abuse occurred or in later years while the priest was still active.

For some, there is documentation to prove it.

For example, Monsignor Alfred Horrigan, the former president of what is now Bellarmine University, said in a recent deposition that the parents of a victim reported her being abused by the Rev. Kevin Cole, a teacher at Bellarmine in the early 1960s.

Horrigan, now 87, said in an interview that he didn't see a need to report Cole's alleged abuse of --------------, who was 6 or 7 at the time, because Cole told him he was seeing a psychiatrist for his problem and Horrigan thought he would get the treatment he needed. Cole is accused of later abusing four other girls.

(Victim's name has been omitted to protect her identity.)

Tiny pieces ... sometimes I feel like I'm going to fly apart into a million tiny shards of glass, each with the smallest reflection of the terror I went through as a child.

I am screaming out in agony.
Will this ever end?

Will there ever be a day when I don't feel as if my body is being ripped apart from the inside out?

Will I ever stop hearing screams of pain, and the whimpering sounds afterwards?

Sometimes I wish I could just let go of it all, but I simply don't know how. It's as much a part of me as my arm or my leg or my hand. I could dismember my whole body, and I would still hear it in my head, even as those dismembered parts feel it in their bones.

Shannon, 2019

Eleven

I don't remember if he raped Sissy first or me. Sissy didn't remember either. It just seemed like all the sudden that it was a new kind of tickle game. One of us would be coloring, and the other would be playing tickle.

He told us he was God's man, and we were God's brides. He said he was giving us God's special love. Only very special girls ever get to have this!

He liked to take pictures of us on the coffee table in his room. He was really happy when Sissy wore her pretty new First Communion dress for a picture. He had one framed for Mommy and Daddy. He took one of me in his favorite dress. He framed that for Mommy and Daddy too.

He made us both wear our First Communion dresses for him every chance he could get. He told Mommy we looked like little brides. He loved to rape us while we were wearing those dresses. And many times, he would light up a cigarette afterwards. I have the cigarette burn holes on my dress from the ashes that fell from his cigarette.

I remember rocking under his desk when Sissy was in the bedroom with him. She would be crying. I would rock back and forth. Back and forth. I was so very scared. Scared because he was hurting my Sissy. But even more, I was terrified because I was next.

I LEARNED TO FLY AWAY WHEN I WAS WITH HIM.

There was a spot on his curtains that I would stare at. If I stared hard enough, I could forget what was happening.

He started making us go to confession. He said we made him do bad things.

He was also invited to many of the family parties with my daddy's family. He was at my aunt's house on Christmas night and would catch me upstairs coming out of the bathroom. He loved giving us special Christmas "presents" there.

He.
Was.
Everywhere.

There was no place during those years where he wouldn't show up. He would help at our church, especially during holidays. We had to take a nap every Christmas Eve a few hours before midnight mass. He was always there to "tuck us in" for that nap.

I can still hear him in my head when he was on the altar. He had a habit of saying "and uh" a lot. I remember him saying that during his homilies.

I remember him saying, "Lord, wash away my iniquities. Cleanse me from my sins." Those words still echo in my head every time I go to mass.

I don't understand how someone could stand on the altar of the Almighty God and consecrate His Body and Blood and then that same person could do what he did to us.

Sometimes while doing the most mundane tasks of life, a button will be pushed, and the rewind tape is engaged. Such was a normal day as I was recently folding laundry.

The grandkids had stayed with us the previous weekend, and among my granddaughter's things were some cute little panties. As I started to fold them, I noticed they had a word printed on them.

Saturday.
Such a simple word. Just a day of the week. No big deal.

I slid to the floor as the tears came. Not again, I thought, not again. Don't go there. It's just a little, simple word.

Fr. Kevin sent us home with new underwear, pretty little panties, from the very first weekend he raped us. He had to because our underwear had blood stains on them. Thinking back on it now, he had to have those cute little panties waiting and ready in his apartment on the Catholic college campus before we got there. He had to have known he would need them from previous times with other little girls. He was prepared.

He called them "Every Day" panties because each pair had a design printed on them with one day of the week. Sunday. Monday. Tuesday. Wednesday. Thursday. Friday.

Saturday.

Fr. Kevin took us home that first weekend and showed our parents our new presents with the days on each pair. The adults had a big laugh about them, and Mom and Dad would tease us each day about having the correct day's underwear on from then on.

As I sat on my laundry room floor and cried, fifty-seven years after that first pair of Saturday panties was given to me, I realized again this will probably happen in different ways and times until I take my last breath. This is when I will have to just keep digging deep for my faith, my strength, and my spirit of endurance. This is what I call a long-haul mentality. It is the only thing I have left to throw when old memories come blowing in.

Shannon, 2021

Twelve

Some people grow up, but Little Shannon never got that opportunity. She has continued to peek from her hiding place when I least expect it, and as you can imagine, as the legal battle with the archdiocese moved through the court system, my everyday life changed dramatically. And so did Little Shannon's.

MY FEELINGS FOR THE CHURCH ITSELF BEGAN TO CHANGE.

Such a feeling of deception. That's the only description I had about the way Archbishop Thomas Kelly had handled cases of abuse for years. As more and more documents were released, my heart broke at the destruction wrought on hundreds of innocent children for so long.

In April 2003, I sent an editorial into our local newspaper, *The Courier Journal*. It was published the day after the Kentucky Derby when the Derby City was full of out-of-town guests. It caused quite a bit of uproar, especially because I asked the archbishop to resign.

In the editorial, I wrote that I was leaving the church and began asking people to sign a petition to encourage the archbishop to resign. I was a spokesperson for the survivors on television and interviewed on radio shows. The abuse cases were big news stories every day. Everywhere I went, people asked about my knowledge of the court cases in Louisville and throughout the country.

The people at the church where I had grown up felt the editorial made them look complicit or possibly just stupid for not knowing what had gone on in their own church. Nothing could have been further from the truth. They were as innocent as Debbie and I were. I mourn the pain the editorial caused them, but I had to do it.

MY BEING PART OF THE LAWSUIT DIDN'T SIT WELL WITH MANY OF MY FRIENDS.

One of my closest friends told me that when I sued the church, I sued him personally. "I didn't give my money to the church to go to someone like you," was a comment I heard often. He—and so many others—had torn a hole in my soul.

My situation at work grew tense, to say the least. I wasn't mentally or emotionally in the best place. I was still on a lot of medications to treat ongoing depression, PTSD, severe anxiety, psychosis, and other things. I was informed by upper management I was not allowed to discuss anything to do with the court case or my abuse at work.

My boss gave me a scripted plan of what I should reply if I was asked about the ongoing lawsuit or my abuse specifically. If I was asked about it, I was told to say that I couldn't comment, which was a challenge since people would see me on the news regularly and want to know. Many times, after someone would continue to question me and I would repeat "No comment," or "I can't comment," my boss would finally come out of his office and tell them that I really was not allowed to comment while at work.

Some coworkers wanted as much information as they could get. Others used my circumstance against me. Some went to my boss and gave him a list of things they did not want *me* to say or do at work because it made *them* uncomfortable, knowing what caused it. At the end of my shift one day, my boss brought their list to me. He told me I needed to follow their list of demands so they wouldn't be uncomfortable working with me. The list included these points:

I WAS NOT ALLOWED TO TALK, OF COURSE, ABOUT ANYTHING HAVING TO DO WITH THE LAWSUITS OR MY ABUSE.

I was not allowed to say I was tired, as it made them think I wouldn't be able to finish out the day. I wasn't allowed to cry or look sad, because they knew what caused it, and it made them uncomfortable. I wasn't allowed to stare off in space, because they knew what I was probably thinking about, and, yep, it made them uncomfortable. Yada, yada, yada. I felt like I'd been slapped in the face. It read like Victim Shaming 101 to me.

When I came back to work on my next scheduled day, I met with my boss. I told him that I would do my best to abide by their requests, but I had requests of my own. He raised his eyebrows as I said that. I then gave him my requests.

They couldn't talk about their alcoholic family members because it made me feel uncomfortable. They couldn't talk about drinking alcohol, as that made me very nervous and uncomfortable. They couldn't talk about being tired and needing a nap after lunch because it made me feel they wouldn't be able to finish out the day.

At this point, my boss broke into a huge grin and told me, "Girl, you've got spunk!" We talked for a while longer about the unknowing cruelty of my peers. He presented my list to them on my next day off, and nothing more was ever said to me about lists of demands.

Sometimes we never see how God answers prayers; this time it was crystal clear.

Not long after, an opening came up at an outpatient imaging center within our parent company. This meant that I was able to get away from the toxic work environment and diminish a major trigger of mine: having male patients. At the outpatient center, I only cared for women. I took that position, and it was the best job I had in my entire career. I spent my last fifteen and a half years there working with the best group of people ever.

Over time, I was able to rebuild relationships with a few of the coworkers from the earlier years, and I cherish them as good friends now.

Editorial May 4, 2003

"A Plea From a Cradle Catholic" by Shannon Shaughnessy Age

I am a "cradle Catholic." My parents brought us up to believe that you never question a priest because he is the next best thing to God.

My family life revolved around St. Luke Church. We lived directly across the street. Dad was in charge of altar boy training, Mom was in the choir, was a cantor, lector and C.C.D. instructor, and was the head of Youth Ministry. My sister was a C.C.D. teacher and became the youth minister when Mom stepped down.

I started a pre-school religion program when I was fourteen years old and was in charge of the program until I was nineteen. I was the seventh and eighth grade cheerleading coach from 1974 until 1981. At my adult parish, St. Bernard, my husband

and I and another couple started a mission group named Sow the Word. We and over one hundred others traveled to Appalachia many weekends for eight years to help at a tuition free college prep school founded in 1990. We worked on that school, worked on homes, served meals, and delivered food.

My son and I represented St. Bernard on the steering committee for the Community Hunger Walk for many years. Our whole family worked at a homeless shelter in the Creation Relation program called Study Buddies. And my sister and I were abuse by Father Kevin Cole for six very long years. The letters recently released, which Archbishop Thomas Kelly wrote in 1983 regarding the abuse perpetrated by Father Tom Creagh was devastating to me, and as a result, my family and I left the Catholic Church last Thursday. Knowing without a doubt that Archbishop Kelly left Father Creagh in service with access to innocent children, I can no longer feel comfortable in this church. Knowing that he described the victim's family as vindictive, and hostile lets me know Archbishop Kelly's true feelings about victims and their families.

Do not let Archbishop Kelly confuse you! He did not turn over the files willingly or cheerfully; he did so only because of a court order. And he has tried to downplay his involvement in the Father Miller cases, too. Archbishop Kelly came to be our leader in 1982, and at that time, inherited all the church files. These files included abuse cases reported by Father Miller from 1957 to the present time. Yet it took Archbishop Kelly eight years to move Father Miller out of the church setting. And where did he move Father Miller? To a nursing home to serve as a chaplain. Father Miller was never supervised on weekends when many grandparents were visited by their grandchildren.

In the case of Father Creagh, Archbishop Kelly knew firsthand of the abuse. Yet, even when the scandal was breaking in Boston, Archbishop Kelly did not remove Father Creagh or any other of the priests in his archdiocese known to have committed abuse. Only after the National Conference of Bishops made it mandatory did Archbishop Kelly remove any of the abusive priests.

My decision to leave the Catholic Church is one that I have struggled with since I began therapy in 1992. At many times, I was unable to attend mass because of memories of the abuse; of being raped by God's man ... who said I was God's bride and only he could show me God's love, of having to go to confession to him at St. Luke's after he had abused me in the sacristy, the confessional, the rectory, or any of the hundreds of other times he abused me from 1964 to 1970. But my faith in the holiness of mass, and especially communion, always brought me back.

When I think of a good shepherd, I think of a person willing to do anything to protect his flock. Archbishop Kelly has time and again shown that the safety of children is less important to him than the reputation of the church. Only now that the abuse issue has been made public knowledge, has he attempted to act like he cares. After reading the documents, I know I will never feel safe in the Catholic Church led by one who has continually put children in danger.

Archbishop, if you truly want to show compassion to the victims, please step down so we can begin to heal.

God,

In quiet moments, I whisper your name. Sometimes in thanksgiving for all the gifts you have given me. Sometimes in exasperation for another project gone awry. Sometimes pleading for you to help me to have the strength just to get through this moment.

God,

I'm finally able to see that you are always here, whether I'm aware of it or not. And I'm sure you get a big kick and chuckle at how I mess up the easiest task possible. I'm also sure that, when I do mess up again, you will be there to help me straighten things out.

God,

I can also see that, no matter how much I want to change people or situations, there are many times when that's just not possible. And I know that in those moments of despair, I can go to you for comfort. You too were neglected by those who should have loved you. You too were hurt by things said about you that weren't true. You too were shunned by family and friends whom you never dreamed would desert you. I don't take comfort in the fact you felt the same pain. No, but I do take comfort in the fact you endured it.

God,

May I always come to you with my joys and my pains. May I always look to you for your wisdom and your strength. May I feel your presence when a task is successfully completed in a gentle, knowing smile. And may I always know you will forever be there to comfort me.

God.

Shannon, August 12, 1994

Thirteen

Trauma impacts more than just the survivor. My family was majorly affected by my being in the public eye because of the lawsuit against the Catholic Church. It affected each of us dramatically in its own way.

FOR MY HUSBAND, STEVE, IT HIT PROFESSIONALLY VERY HARD.

Steve was a senior program manager with a facilities development firm. At the time of the lawsuit, his major project, worth in the tens of millions of dollars, was with a religious order and Catholic college in rural Kentucky, and they just loved Steve. He had been on the project for several years, and the project was running under budget and ahead of schedule. In addition, his other projects gave nothing but positive reviews about Steve.

Within weeks of my editorial being published in the newspaper in May 2003, Steve was all the sudden in hot water at his firm. They never could tell him exactly what he was doing wrong, only that he needed to do better. The clients told him they had no problems with the way work was being done. Nonetheless, in September 2003, Steve's position was eliminated, and the career he loved was destroyed. He was devastated. He loved his job. He loved his clients. All of that was ripped from him. After several years trying to regain his status in his career field, he finally moved on and let it go.

OUR SONS HAD THEIR OWN PROBLEMS TO DEAL WITH.

Our oldest, Austin, said little but was always at my side. Years later, he shared with us how he felt he had to become my parent. What a horrible burden for a sixteen-year-old to have to bear. It changed the dynamics of our relationship.

Patrick, at the time, was a student at a Catholic middle school. Evidently, his mother suing the church was a topic of discussion among his classmates. He was teased about it, and at one point, one of his "friends" said, "I heard your mom used to f&$@ a priest. Is that true?" My heart was broken for him.

Even to this day, both of my sons bear so much trauma and pain, not only from my journey of healing throughout their whole lives, but also from the public display of the lawsuit.

I sometimes wonder if it was worth it to join the lawsuit, which exposed my family to so much pain so publicly. I am proud of the changes that have come to our Catholic Church because we, as a group of survivors, fought and changed the way abuse is now handled. I am also proud of the laws we were able to change in Kentucky following the lawsuit protecting children from sexual abuse.

But most things come at a cost, and sometimes it feels as if the price to my family has been too much to pay.

Today has been a good day. Steve was offered and accepted a new job. It's so good to feel like security is back in our lives. I'm so proud of him—he's the love of my life!

The meds I'm taking are making me a little dizzy and jumpy, but that's better than having delusions. Wednesday, I felt like everything was short circuiting. I couldn't get to B from A without going to Z first. At least I am no longer planning to "cut all the bad spots" out of me.

The boys are no longer boys. In two weeks, Austin will be nineteen. Patrick is fifteen. They both are such a joy. I love the men they are becoming.

My sweet Callie girl is sleeping under my bed as I write. I feel as if she's the little girl I lost, in dog form. She's so affectionate and trusting. She just wants love—no more; no less. She's precious.

For tonight, the devil is at bay. I'm stronger than he likes me to be but weaker than I like to be. Strength is measured first by the minute, then the hour, then the day.

Today has been a good day.

Shannon, October 8, 2004

Fourteen

My price to pay was also very demanding—more than I had expected.

In 2002, the attorney representing us had my sister and me undergo a comprehensive psychological assessment for use in the court case against the Archdiocese of Louisville. It was a necessary but grueling two-day assessment.

We first were put through all the usual tests used in this type of work up —from countless questionnaires to in-person interrogation. I remember the written questions seemed to go on for hours. We then went back for a face-to-face meeting with the psychologist and her associate. I was in panic mode during this part of the testing, bringing to light everything I had tried so hard to bury, so they allowed Debbie to stay with me.

In June 2003, I was given a copy of the report. It was very in depth. For the first time ever, I felt validation for what the abuse had caused in my everyday life. However, it was hard to realize that someone could choose to leave such devastation behind without a second thought for what he had done to me.

The following is directly taken from the diagnostic impressions and recommendations from this June 6, 2003, report.

Shannon Age is 42-year-old women with a history of frequent and continuous sexual abuse from the ages of four to ten. Over this six-year period, Fr. Kevin Cole took egregious advantage of Shannon's family friendship an estimated 200 to 300 times. This sexual abuse is a substantial factor in Shannon's personality disorder and the post-traumatic stress disorder, both of which have become lifelong conditions. Since Shannon was a preschool child when he began to molest her, Fr. Cole's almost absolute control and frequent abuse created an environment of inescapable terror for this developing child. Such frightening, intense experiences led to the establishment of an emotionally chaotic inner life for Shannon, which results in the unstable sense of self and others that characterizes a personality disorder. Due to Fr. Cole, Shannon has developed a pattern of dissociated effect, regression under stress, and dramatic mood changes that make it difficult for her to function with stability now. She panics easily and responds dramatically to stressful situations that others might handle with equanimity. She is preoccupied with the abuse that she has suffered because she still experiences many intrusive symptoms. It will take many years for her to resolve these problems.

Shannon has been in psychotherapy for 11 years, yet she still experiences suicidal tendencies and dissociative episodes. Like many people with severe trauma and a personality disorder, she is likely to require many years of psychotherapy and psychiatric treatment. To her credit, Shannon is courageously attempting to take appropriate action in speaking out clearly against the system which perpetuated Fr. Cole's pedophilic activities. Her struggle to help herself and other victims through political activism is a strength. Shannon should be afforded the opportunity to obtain up to 10 more years of mental health treatment of her choice. Such long treatment will be necessary to help her establish a stable sense of self and to develop emotional equilibrium.

Some days, the pain and anxiety from those early years come screaming in and take root in all that I have tried to rebuild.

Nothing new or specifically triggering that I can pinpoint; and yet all I want to do is run and hide. PTSD sucks. Memories, flashbacks, smells, sounds all come rushing back. Most days, I can push it back in the box, shut the lid, and go on with my life. Now and then, though, it just sucker punches you and takes you down for the count.

And so, Little Shannon is curling up in Jesus's lap for a nap now. Only He can protect me from those old days. I am going to stop running and just rest in His Holy arms.

Shannon, February 2022

Fifteen

In 1992, when I first began to piece together my memories of the abuse, I found it almost unbearable to be in a church. Constant flashbacks throughout mass brought back how much the theology used in mass was, many times, the things Fr. Kevin said or did while abusing us. The fact he so closely tied our First Communion dresses, worn as "God's brides," to his sexual foreplay made the sacrament that brought me to church and my most cherished sacrament almost unbearable. And yet, it *was* that very sacrament which brought me to church, many times with tears rolling down my face. I truly didn't feel whole without the Eucharist.

IN 2002, WHEN THE LAWSUIT AGAINST THE ARCHDIOCESE BEGAN, ALL THAT AGONY WAS BACK WITH A NEW FORCE, BUT THIS TIME IN A MUCH MORE PUBLIC WAY.

Now, *everyone* knew why I was so tearful and distraught when I went to mass. And, as one who was suing the church, there were now members who blamed us, the victims, for all the turmoil. I was a victim of some of the most heinous crimes that could be committed against a child, and yet I felt as if *I* were on trial.

My pastor at the time told me I already had my chance to speak to the media. He, as did most of the priests in Louisville, felt we were wrong in calling for the archbishop to resign. We as victims not only had to bear our memories of the actual abuse, but we also had to endure the very church we loved blaming us for wanting justice. For many years (and even to this day), people would ask me why I didn't find another denomination to fill my spiritual needs so I wouldn't have to go through this kind of torture every time I walked into the church.

I tried. The problem with that idea was that this church, this broken and battered church, was the only way I could get my spiritual needs met. My soul cried out for the Holy Eucharist, even if I had to go through flashbacks to get to the altar. It was the only time I felt God's loving hands on my heart and soul, even as I cried.

As much as I tried to stay away, I found I simply could not. By early summer of 2003, I began going back to mass from time to time. I needed —no, I craved—the Holy Eucharist. Without it, I was just lost. And with so many other parts of me lost, I couldn't let this part of me be lost too.

In July 2003, we were at mass when a retired, former pastor of our parish was there to fill in. He started his homily, and I am paraphrasing from so long ago.

If a man has a few beers, that doesn't make him an alcoholic. If a man smokes a few cigarettes, that doesn't mean he's addicted to nicotine. And if a man abuses a couple of kids, that doesn't make him a pedophile.

As a gasp went up in the congregation, tears started rolling down my face. Steve and I stood, motioned to the boys to stand too, and our family walked out of *that* church.

Afterward, Steve started attending a different Catholic church closer to our home. I didn't want to leave our parish of eighteen years, but I knew I had to, as I tried to go back one or two more times but cried through the mass.

In September 2003, we joined our new parish.

I feel like I am drowning.

Sometimes, I feel like the sadness deep in my soul would surely drown me if I ever opened that door. Little Shannon is so scared and alone. I want to hold her and comfort her, but it feels like I would shatter and no longer exist if I try to open the door again. I feel her pain and anguish with my every breath.

Little One, the bad people are all dead, and yet you never forget what they did. I wish rocking you would console you.

I wish I could chase those memories away forever.
I wish you could know the love God meant for you and not what you were shown.

I believe seeing all the kids in their First Communion pictures with the little girls in their dresses brought back the whole, "I am God's man, you are God's bride, and this is God's love" speech from Fr. Kevin.

Dear Jesus and Mary, please take it away!

Shannon, May 2017

Sixteen

Fourteen months. It felt like eternity. A lifetime. From the first Louisville lawsuit until the settlement agreement was finalized between the Archdiocese and the legal team of the survivors took every bit of this time. And it took another eight months afterward to decide the details of each claim and disbursements of the settlement among the 243 of us.

I had a sense of closure, but trauma, unfortunately, didn't recognize it. I continued to look for ways to overcome my past, or at least learn to live with it without retraumatizing myself.

A few years later, a group of survivors—myself included—went to a nearby monastery in Gethsemane, Kentucky, for a visit with the monks.

Most monks live a quiet, solitary, and cloistered lifestyle. There is peace in that, and I was searching for peace. We all were.

This was the monastery where Fr. Thomas Merton lived and died. He was one of the preeminent American Catholic thought leaders, having written more than fifty books on spirituality, social justice, and pacifism during his life.

In preparation for our visit, the survivors were asked to send the monks awaiting our arrival something to help them to understand what our abuse had caused in our lives. They were open to hearing and to help us heal. I sent a video I was a part of that had been recorded in Texas a few years prior about clergy abuse survivors that was created for distribution to the Order priests.

Linkup was an organization that advocated for clergy abuse victims. Headquartered in Chicago, it moved to Louisville as the cases kept breaking there. Per capita, the Archdiocese of Louisville had more cases of clergy abuse than any other area in the US, even more than in Boston. It was this organization that organized the video I was a part of and shared with the monks.

Because we wanted the monks to understand our abuse had affected more than just us, we brought our family members along with us. We attended vespers, a meaningful prayer service in preparation for mass, which we also attended with the monks. Afterward, we joined together in a large room where we all shared stories—survivors and families of the survivors. I shared my story, and my husband and sons shared theirs of how my abuse affected and changed their lives too.

The monks were given permission to verbally ask us questions, which was unique since they typically lived their lives with moments of silence. There was so much dialogue, laughter, and tears. And there was heartbreak. For some, there was healing.

As the day was waning, the monks shared a meal with us. There was so much sharing of thoughts and hearts and sorrow and joy. There was hugging and hand holding.

I think God, and maybe Fr. Thomas Merton as well, was smiling that day.

WE ARE THE BODY OF CHRIST ...

And today, you will find us in the Garden of Gethsemane with our Lord and Savior, who is in anguish. Jesus, who took the scourging, the crown of thorns, and the crucifixion for our sins, is weeping with tears of His Most Precious Blood.

He weeps for those who have been abused by His clergy. He weeps for their families and loved ones. He cries out in agony because of the ones who took His sacred trust and abused His innocent children. He cries out in pain because of those who were called to lead and nurture His flock, but instead chose to cover up again and again for the very ones who were damaging His children. He yearns to hold His clergy that are innocent, but yet will be judged because of those who have so arrogantly sinned.

As I kneel next to my Jesus in Gethsemane, we give comfort to each other. He holds me tenderly, and I tell my Jesus that, despite what the evil ones have done, we are STILL HIS BODY ON EARTH. We are His, because He chose us, and He is first, and always, ours!

So what must we do as THE BODY OF CHRIST? First, we must thank God for His Church here on earth. We must thank Him for His many blessings. We must be Christ for all who are wounded!

Next, we must pray fervently for His whole Church. We are all sinners with a multitude of varying sins. We must remember that we sin anytime we choose our will, our way, over God's will and way. The arrogance of God's people is almost always their downfall. So, pray.

Pray for the victims of abuse.
Pray for those clergy who are suffering innocently.
Pray for those who are guilty of either the abuse or the cover-ups.
Pray for their conversion.
Pray for our local bishop, Archbishop Joseph Kurtz.
Pray that God will grant him wisdom, patience, tenderness, and compassion as he helps his flock to trust and heal.
Pray for our priests, deacons, sisters and lay ministers.
Pray that the sins of the few will not shake the faith of the Church.
Talk with God. Share with Him your pain and anger. Let Him hold you tenderly in His holy arms.

And NEVER forget ...

WE ARE THE BODY OF CHRIST!

Shannon, August 2018

Seventeen

I've always been a fair person, and this situation deserves fairness too. Every story has two sides, and for that reason, I feel the need to address the late Archbishop Thomas Kelly, who I had requested to resign from his position.

As you have probably surmised, I was not a fan of his. I feel, as it pertains to clergy abuse, he grossly abused his powers. Furthermore, he also personally said things to me that were horrid.

AFTER THE CASES WERE SETTLED, ARCHBISHOP KELLY AGREED TO MEET WITH STEVE AND ME AT HIS OFFICE SO I COULD HAVE AN HONEST CONVERSATION WITH HIM.

It just so happened that I was recovering from bronchitis and had very little speaking voice on that day. When the Archbishop greeted us, I whispered that I was sorry that I could barely speak. His response was, and I quote, "God does answer prayers." Perhaps he thought he was being humorous, but this was no situation for sarcasm.

We sat in his office, uncomfortable but necessary, and talked for quite a while. I showed him the pictures and letters from Fr. Kevin that my family had, proving the path of a pedophile. I wanted him to see the full extent of what one looked like up close and personal.

I asked the archbishop something that was heavy on my heart. I wondered why he had, I felt, lied so often to the press saying that, because of the lawsuits, churches, services, and jobs would be closed and lost. This wasn't a fair statement; while parts of it may have been accurate, the purpose behind it wasn't the lawsuit, but the lack of addressing the abuse over the course of decades.

He stood strong that the statements were not lies. I stood just as strong, telling him, "Yes, they are. If the victims had been taken care of properly, and the abusers had not been allowed to keep re-abusing, there would have never been any lawsuits."

Archbishop Kelly patted my hand and said with a little grin, "My dear, I think you are just a little too sensitive."

I had hoped for some form of reconciliation in that meeting, but his statement robbed me of that. A week or so after that meeting, he sent a warm thank you note. He thanked me for sharing my pain and memories with him and said he would continue to keep me in his prayers. While I was still hurt, I was touched by his kindness in sending the note.

Having said all this, it still would not be right to judge the late archbishop by only one, horrible as it was, aspect of his tenure as archbishop. I am told he was a very humble and loved leader. And so, let me give you a glimpse of this leader who made so many decisions that affected so many victims in my locale. It is written by Dr. Brian Reynolds, Chancellor of the Archdiocese of Louisville, someone who knew him well, and perhaps understood his reasons for doing things the way he did.

* * *

I first met Archbishop Thomas Kelly O.P. in 1980, the year before he became Archbishop of Louisville. During the 1980s I worked as a consultant to several agencies of the Archdiocese and in 1990 he asked me to join the staff full time. Over the next decade, I worked with him almost every day. I was with him in wonderful, exciting times but also in difficult days. Those years involved the renovation of the Cathedral and opening of new parishes, but there were also parish closings and agency consolidations, which most everyone saw as necessary but required very painful decisions and processes.

Kelly, as most people referred to him, had more than one health crisis, including having half of a lung removed. Recovery from that surgery contributed to the surfacing of his addiction to alcohol followed by a very public admission and then months of treatment. I got to know the vulnerable man, Thomas Kelly, in very personal ways over these years.

It is with this backdrop I share a few reflections on Archbishop Kelly as he responded to the reality of sexual abuse by priests in the Archdiocese of Louisville. Shannon asked me to share some thoughts, which is a testament to her belief that everyone in this terrible experience of abuse has a personal story.

It would perhaps take an entire book to share all my thoughts but let me limit myself to three. I offer these notes not to defend or explain his actions but to give some insight to what I believe he experienced.

First, as an archbishop he took his role as a father figure to his priests as the highest priority and first responsibility. While it is true, he was Shepherd to all the faithful of the archdiocese, as their bishop he saw caring for his priests much as any parent cares for their children. Even when they did something wrong, he first sought to let them feel loved and accepted without exception. Because of this, when learning about a report of abuse of a child, his first thought was of all the good the priest had done and how he could not reconcile what he was hearing about them as an abuser with his belief in their goodness.

Second, Archbishop Kelly was frankly somewhat naive about child abuse and sexual matters. He was a well-trained, highly educated cleric who grew up with only one sibling and with a mother who spent a number of years as a single parent. He entered religious life while a very young adult. He often told me he could not imagine a priest hurting a child and was shocked to hear the forms of abuse that occurred.

Finally, Archbishop Kelly loved the Church as a community but also as an institution. He worried that the sins of a few could bring great scandal to the Church. I believe those sins scandalized him. While clearly wrong in hindsight, somehow, he thought if no one knew what occurred it would prevent pain and preserve the believers trust in their faith. In almost any decision he made he would always ask, often out loud, what will happen to the people? So, his love for priests, his naive view of some matters, and his fear of scandal led this man who I knew to have great compassion to miss the main issue of the abuse crisis.

Young children were being hurt and the pain and damage they experienced needed his clear, swift leadership response to help stop and prevent it. While he knew of some cases of abusive priests, he did not know there were hundreds of children abused in this archdiocese.

As he began to learn that truth in 2002 to 2003, he became a different bishop and priest. I was with him as he slowly accepted the imperfections of priests he loved and signed papers that they be removed from ministry or saw them sent to prison. I sat with him as he met with victim survivors and heard their cries. His efforts to apologize for what someone did or what he failed to do, were rarely accepted. He came to see it was too late or too little for many. This was a weight he carried to his final days.

I do know how deeply he wanted healing and how easily he accepted legal settlements, saying the victims deserved support. He prayed deeply for those who were hurt. Strange as it may seem, I do believe Archbishop Kelly and Shannon Age could have helped each other. Both needed healing; both would have benefited.

Dr. Brian Reynolds
Ed.D., Chancellor/Chief Administrative Officer for the Archdiocese of Louisville

I'm feeling that ache again.
The ache of a child abandoned.
No one to hold me, to protect me, to stop the pain.

The evil one is haunting me again. I can't see him, yet I know he's there. He's waiting for me to be still. He's waiting for me to sleep. That is where he's most at home.

I drift off to sleep, and he is giving me a bath. The bathtub has a steep angle at the end that lets me slide down and into the water. I land with a splash, and we laugh. Then, it's time to wash. He washes my face and gets behind my ears. Then comes my arms, chest, and back. Then my toes are next, and he counts them and tickles them. I squeal with delight. Then he washes my legs and bottom-and I start to tense. I hope this time he doesn't clean me really good. But, oh, he likes his girls to be clean "inside and out."

And so, it starts. He wipes hard with a rag. Then he says, "It's time to clean inside."

I beg him not to, 'cause it hurts, and the soap burns. But he reminds me that only bad girls are stinky. Bad girls smell like baby pants. His girls always smell good, like soap.

And I softly cry.

Shannon, 2022

Eighteen

Sexual abuse in different situations can cause very different outcomes. Let me explain.

Through the decades, starting in the 1990s, I attended multiple retreats and conferences on sexual abuse to help my healing journey. Some of these were specifically for clergy abuse survivors, while some were for any victims of abuse. I have numerous friends, family members, coworkers and acquaintances who were sexually abused as children. We share many symptoms, triggers and coping mechanisms. Most have had some, if not years, of therapy. Many who were abused by family members were ostracized by other family members for naming their abuser. Many victims have been disowned by their families for "causing problems" for the abusing family member whom everyone knew about but no one had ever had the courage to stop.

BEING A VICTIM OF CLERGY ABUSE HAS ITS UNIQUE PROBLEMS.

After my abuse was public, I was blamed for people losing jobs in the archdiocese and for churches being closed. I was told to pray for healing.

I was told that others were praying for me. Sometimes that was a comfort. Other times, it felt like a slap in the face.

Remember, my abuser was "God's man."

God's man—using the sacraments of Holy Eucharist, reconciliation, and penance—left deep scars on my soul.

Though I say The Lord's Prayer almost every day, words like Father and God can knock me down. When I read that the church is Jesus's bride, it brings back such terrible pain, because I was told *I* was God's bride by my abuser.

For many years after I started therapy, I still was faithful, but my prayer life was practically nonexistent. How could I find the courage to pray to God, after what happened with God's man? How could I pray to Jesus? After all, he is still a man, and most men scare the hell out of me. I really didn't have much of a sense of the Holy Spirit, so I never went down that avenue.

I finally found my God in the Garden of Gethsemane, in agony, praying to His Father. This is where I feel at home with God. I can relate to this God, this Jesus in agony, and this image. This is where I finally allowed Jesus into my pain, even as He was on His way to Calvary. In my days of deepest despair, I know that Jesus in the garden is down in the deepest of the muck with me. And I also know that he is going on to the Resurrection in three days, and I will be there with him to celebrate.

Just move on ...

I have been told by so many people in so many ways that I should just let go of the past, move on, and get over it. Such trite little sayings. Oh, how I wish those speaking these words knew how harmful their comments are to me and those like me. Do they think a person wants to stay stuck in this pain for their entire life?

Yesterday, I woke up remembering the nightmare that had just happened in my sleep. I tried to push it away because it was Sunday and I needed to get ready for a long morning at church. It was Steve's weekend to preach, so we would have to be at church early. I was to lector at the second mass that day. The readings were good, about the Ten Commandments and Jesus cleaning out the temple and overturning the money changers' tables. As the deacon, Steve had written a wonderful homily, and I was looking forward to being at church with him.

As we usually do when I am to read at church, I practiced on the drive there. After the fourth time, I paused and told Steve I had had another nightmare and was shaken about it. He asked if I wanted to talk about it, and so I started.

Adult Shannon was in bed with Fr. Kevin, and I was trying to get his driver's license out of his hand. I knew he should be almost ninety-three years old, just like my mom would be in a few weeks if she were still alive. The Fr. Kevin in my dream kept laughing and putting the license just out of my reach so I couldn't see the date of birth. He looked so young to me—

the same hairy chest, the same body—but I somehow knew he should be old. I finally saw the date of birth, but it had been scratched out.

My deacon husband, who was about to vest up as clergy and walk up on the altar, held my hand, and told me he loved me. I could see the pain in his eyes as he listened to my nightmare.

The first mass went well. Steve's homily was well received. I received the Lord in the Eucharist and was fed. We talked to people after mass and then went to the rectory for a few minutes before the second mass. I had a "cuppa hot tea," like the Irish gal I am, and went back over to church for the second mass.

About ten minutes before the second mass was to start, I went to sit down in church. As I was sitting there by myself, the rest of the nightmare came to me.

I heard my mom call from outside the room, and Fr. Kevin threw back the covers and got up. He was completely naked. He went out of the room, and I could hear him and Mom talking and laughing.

Of course, that was just a nightmare. It didn't happen. But as I sat in church, I felt as if the devil himself was trying to get hold of my stomach. I thought I was going to throw up.

It was less than five minutes to the start of mass. My husband was getting ready to walk down the aisle. I was supposed to go up and proclaim God's Word, and I was sure I was going to throw up. So instead, I went to the statue of the Blessed Mother, begged her and Jesus and a legion of angels to accompany me up on the altar, said the Hail Mary, and went back to my seat and sat. I wiped away my tears and watched Steve and our pastor process down the aisle.

When it was time, Mother Mary, Jesus, a legion of angels, and I went up on the altar, and I proclaimed the Word of God. I went back to my seat, wiped away a few more tears, thanked God, Jesus, and Mother Mary. Later that afternoon, I told Steve and two of our dearest friends the whole story. Steve smiled at me and told me the altar had felt a little more crowded than usual.

My point to all of this is, just how do you ever get over something that attacks you in your sleep? Or grabs you because of something you smell, or hear, or taste or see that brings you back to a horrible memory from fifty plus years ago? If I had been horribly burned in a fire as a child and had burn scars all over my body, I am sure no one would have the audacity to tell me to just get over it. Instead, I carry the internal scars of so many rapes, sodomies, and other brutalities, and I am expected to just get over it.

Well, it ain't happening in my dreams, but maybe it can in yours.

Shannon, 2019

Nineteen

One of the things that still can bring me moments of pain, anger, and disbelief is the program Debbie got from Fr. Kevin's funeral through the provincial vicar at Mt. St. Francis in the 1990's. It was written by his siblings, of which at least his brother, the monsignor, knew of the abuse Fr. Kevin had perpetrated on so many children. It brings that same old gut punch every time I read it, especially one specific paragraph.

> "There was an elderly man in Kevin's nursing home who would unceasingly roll himself around in his wheelchair; and he would work himself thru all sorts of obstacles (chairs, tables, TV sets, whatever): and Kevin was that way with life. He had trouble from his addictions; and 'friends' (he often didn't think so!) would send him to 'Charm School' for a while & get him re-aligned. And Kevin would 'graduate & become a wholesome, working, and happy person again. Relapses would occur, but he would go back to work, getting whole again."

I very much doubt it ever crossed his siblings' minds how any of his victims would feel reading those words. You see, we, his victims, were his worst "addiction." Many of us were abused during his "relapses." "Charm school might have seemed like it made Kevin into a wholesome person, but the shattered bodies, spirits, and souls of his victims tells a very different story. We weren't an obstacle course to maneuver through, we were little malleable children that he devoured and destroyed.

In his death, I pray with my whole heart his demons have finally been slain by the One Holy and Eternal God.

Eternal rest grant unto him, O Lord.
And let the perpetual light shine upon him.

How do you separate the good from the bad?

How do you reconcile that someone who did so many evil things to so many little girls was also someone's beloved brother and son?

These are some of the questions I will forever toss around in my head. For as much harm as he did do, there were tiny sparks of a good, fun person in him that his family remembered.

What I do know is I have a choice.
And with that choice, I chose to let his guilt be addressed by a loving, merciful God.

While I may always have some questions, there is one question I will never ask ... will he be treated mercifully by God? Because I know God, I know Fr. Kevin is exactly where God wants him to be. What a blessing indeed!

Shannon, undated

Twenty

Some days are just hard. This one day was especially hard for me.

The greatest gift my parents gave me is my faith in God. Without it, I would not have survived. I believe that to my core. It is a part of the fiber of who I am. It defines how I make everyday choices in my life. It gives reason to my being. And yet ...

I AM MY MOTHER'S DAUGHTER.

We rarely saw eye to eye. We both felt the other's way of life was wrong. Not "damn you to hell" kind of wrong, just "I won't live that way" kind of wrong. It went without saying that Sissy would always be her favorite and first choice. That was old news to me. When that began to carry over to my children—her grandchildren—I couldn't stay silent anymore. We became more and more rigid in our firmly held lines as the years went by, and the distance between us grew and grew.

Mom had a massive heart attack on New Year's Day, 2001, a year before the lawsuits began. Over the next five days, she put up a strong fight. While she was still conscious but, on a ventilator, Steve encouraged me to tell Mom I was sorry for any and everything I had done to her and that I forgave her everything. Steve felt, and rightly so, I would forever regret it if I didn't tell her this while she could hear and grasp it. Mom wept as she nodded her head that she understood what I had said. It was hard, because at that time, I hadn't truly gotten to a point of forgiveness towards my mother. In addition, I felt the many struggles of our relationship were not only my fault, but hers too.

In retrospect, I am glad I told her. However, to this day, my relationship with my mother, as with my father, takes me back and forth in emotions.

Seeing them one minute as parents who loved their children, and the next as parents who allowed us to be put in such dangerous and damaging circumstances always leaves me confused and perplexed. In many ways, I think my mother either didn't get, or simply wouldn't accept, her part in letting the abuse happen. Her responses were many times what one would expect from a child, not a mother.

On January 6, 2001, on the advice of her many doctors, I decided to stop all life support and let Mom go home to God. Not a day goes by that I don't question that decision—one I had to make as her healthcare surrogate—no matter how many times I have been told by doctors, clergy, my family and so many others that it was the right decision. Making that decision will always haunt me, even if it was the right one.

AND WHAT, AFTER ALL THESE YEARS, HAVE I LEARNED?

I believe I have learned to love more deeply and to mourn more deeply. My sons would probably tell you their mom is still too rigid. I believe I see the love of God in the eyes of little children. I believe I see the yearning for God in those who are sick or in their last days.

And I am learning to believe my mom loved me as best she could.

A dear friend who knew our family so very well in those early years once told me something that has helped me so much. She said simply, "Your mom loved you differently." I think that was a word I've needed to hear for so long—*differently*. I feel that one simple word fills so many holes in my little child's heart. Mommy loved me too, just differently.

God bless you, Barbie, for that healing word!
What a gift you have given me!

Rest in peace, Mom!

Fr. Kevin loved to take pictures of us, and he took them all the time. His favorite place to take them was with one of us posing sitting on his coffee table in front of the closed curtains in his apartment. He gave two pictures that he took of us to my father, which Daddy took with him when he was stationed in Japan in 1969.

While Daddy was in Japan, he had a Japanese artist, using those pictures as a guide, paint a picture of Debbie and me onto China plates. He also had a plate painted with a wedding picture of Mom and him.

When Daddy got home from Japan, he gave those painted China plates to Mom, and she proudly displayed them on the top shelf of her China cabinet.

In 1993, after Debbie started therapy, Debbie asked Mom to take our plates down from display in the China cabinet because of the horrible memories they caused her every time she saw them. Mom told her she loved them because Daddy had had them painted especially for her to put in her China cabinet to show her family. Debbie tried to explain how traumatizing it was for her to have to see those plates every time she came to Mom's house, but Mom would not budge. Dad gave them to her, they were hers, and it was her house. Debbie cried, but Mom stood firm. I truly believe my mother could not, or would not, process how those images on those plates affected us. Was that because of her naivety, or simply denial? I will never know. Either way, I still forgive her.

In 2001, after Mom's death, one of the first things Debbie did was to remove those plates from the China cabinet. They now sit on the bottom shelf of my China cabinet, behind a wooden door.

Why, you may wonder, have I kept them all these years later? I sometimes pull them out and look at the innocent little girls looking back from those old plates.

I can't part with them, because they are a testament to the little girls that made it out of that room. On my worst days, I want to scream and bust those plates into a million pieces. But on my best days, I want to show them off and say, "Look how far I've come!!"

Shannon, 2019

Twenty-One

W hile Debbie and I went through our abuse together, how we each managed it was very different.

From the outside looking in, most anyone who knew Debbie and me would say we were different in every way. I was five foot four inches tall. Debbie was four foot eight and one-half inches. (And don't you ever forget that half inch!) She was blond. I had very dark hair. Her hair was fine, thin and very straight. Mine was super curly and thick.

BUT OUR DIFFERENCES DIDN'T STOP THERE.

I am a neat freak. Debbie hated to clean and rarely did. I loved vegetables; Debbie hated them. Many a night when we were growing up, Debbie would sit at the kitchen table staring at her plate with vegetables on it. She would finally be sent to bed, only to find that Dad had put those same vegetables out for her breakfast. Somehow, Mom would get rid of them while Dad was at work and we were at school.

I tried to have total control over all areas of my life. I had a plan for every day. During high school, I kept a detailed list of exactly what I wore each day to school so as not to repeat the exact same outfit too close together.

I bought most of my clothes with money I earned babysitting, and while they weren't the best, I still tried to be as stylish as I could afford.

I saved my money like a miser. I was so afraid of not having enough money to pay for things I needed. I saved enough money in eleven months with my first job to buy a used car, all the uniforms I would need, and my schoolbooks for X-ray school.

Debbie was freer with her money and enjoyed buying things for herself and others, including me.

After we both married, it seemed like we each continued with our different ways of living; not one better than the other, just different.

Debbie had always remembered everything that had happened to us because she was older. She told me after many years of therapy that she felt guilty for what happened to me.

She never accepted that our parents should have been the ones to protect us, not my six-year-old big sister. I think that was why she bought me so many things before I left home to get married. I guess at that point in her life, she felt she owed me.

Dad had intensified his strict treatment of Debbie after I got married. He constantly ridiculed her, calling her names and generally making her life a living hell. Finally, one night, after he had consumed quite a bit of alcohol, he started up on Debbie again. This time, Mom defended Debbie. Dad went a little crazy and started screaming at both, saying he couldn't believe Mom would go against him. According to both Mom and Debbie, Dad grabbed Debbie around the neck and tried to choke her.

Mom was finally able to pull Dad off, and Mom kicked him out of the house. He went to his oldest sister's house. His sister didn't ask any questions. After sleeping his liquor off, he woke up and went downstairs to the kitchen where his sister was waiting for him. She told him she didn't want to know why he had showed up at her house the night before, but it was time for him to go home and fix his problems. He went home.

Though he still taunted Debbie with ridicule, he never laid a hand on her again.

IN THE FALL OF 1983, DEBBIE MET KENNY.

Kenny made Debbie shine with his love and affection. He was such a wonderful, sweet soul. With his care, Debbie blossomed as never before. Debbie and Kenny got engaged and were married on Friday, July 13, 1984.

But Kenny became ill in 2004. He struggled with illness after illness until 2009. He fought the good fight, but his body could not overcome so many major illnesses at one time. Kenny died in February 2009. My Sissy was worn out from the long illness and devastated by Kenny's death. She floundered in her overwhelming grief.

Her son and daughter-in-law lived with her until a few weeks before their son—her first grandson—was born in December 2013. As they moved into their new home, my sister was for the first time in her life, living alone. She found it unbearable.

After living alone for a year, Debbie decided she wanted to venture into dating again. Kenny had been the one true love of her life; I was amazed she would want to try the dating scene. But then I became hopeful. Maybe if she could find a stable man, she would settle into a healthy life-style and learn to find happiness.

On Christmas Eve, 2014, Debbie told me she had met a man and she was in love. She told me their relationship, thus far, had been totally online. He was in the army and was stationed in Afghanistan. He assured her that when he got out in the spring, he was coming home to her. According to him, he lived in Texas and had a teenage son. They would move to Louisville and become a family.

As I listened to her story, it just didn't ring true. I talked to her children about it, and they told me they were scared for Debbie's safety. It seemed she was on multiple dating apps online and was being contacted by several men who needed her to help them with financial problems. I reached out to Debbie's best friend, too, and the same story was confirmed. An online search proved that this man was indeed a scammer. He had taken thousands of dollars from unsuspecting lonely women.

Debbie was devastated and would not believe that her new love was not for real. She started staying up all night looking at online dating sites for a replacement.

In February 2015, her kids reached out to me wanting to stage an intervention for their mother. They were scared for health and her safety. So, we all showed up to Debbie's house unannounced. When I walked in, I was shocked as I hadn't been inside her home for a few months. She had one lamp turned on in the whole house. She looked as if she hadn't bathed in days. The house was filthy and reeked of cat urine. She was sitting on the couch, online.

She immediately asked us if this was an intervention. I told her she could call it whatever she wanted. We were simply there because we were worried about her. She started crying, telling us we didn't understand how very alone and lonely she was. I had never seen her this low. She told us she just wanted to die. She hated living alone. She felt her life was worthless.

We told her how important she was to us. We told her that she had a wonderful grandson who adored her. She kept saying it didn't matter. She just wanted it all to end.

I asked her what she wanted her legacy to be. What did she want to be remembered for? Didn't she want to see her grandson grow up? Didn't she know that her kids loved her and would be devastated with the death of their only remaining parent? She just kept telling us that we didn't understand.

After talking for an hour or more, we felt we had done and said all we could. She promised she would try to take better care of herself and stop looking for men in the wrong places. We left her with heavy hearts, unsure if we believed her.

A few weeks later, Debbie called me and told me she was going to the airport to meet a man she had met online. She sounded so excited and was telling me she had fixed her hair and even put makeup on. She hadn't done that in years. I called her kids to find out what they knew. They decided that their mom was putting herself in grave danger. They agreed to take her to the airport, but instead took her to the hospital for a psych evaluation.

WHEN SHE REALIZED WHY THEY HAD BROUGHT HER TO THE HOSPITAL, SHE SAT SCREAMING IN THE WHEELCHAIR, REFUSING TO MOVE.

When she finally allowed the hospital personnel to take her just to check her out, she tried to make it seem as if the kids were being outrageous. At about that time, her phone went off with a message from the man she was to have met. He said he hadn't been able to get on his plane to Louisville because of problems with his passport. He needed her to wire him $5,000 to get the correct documents so he could come and meet her. When she said she couldn't, he started cussing her and told her he would never come to see her. Debbie became distraught. The nurses witnessed it, and realized Debbie was in a very scary place emotionally and mentally. They admitted her for a seventy-two-hour psych observation period.

I went to see Debbie two days after her admission, and she was furious with all of us, but especially me. She couldn't understand why I had turned on her. She felt we were all being cruel to her by keeping her from finding her life.

On the day of her release, my niece, nephew, and I were told we needed to be present with her therapist for her exit interview session. When we entered the room, my sister was sitting at the end of the table with the therapist next to her. The three of us sat down on the other side. The therapist explained that Debbie needed to tell us some things so we could better understand where she was in her life. And then she started.

She started with how unfair her life had been. Fr. Kevin had ruined us. Daddy loved me more than her. As she screamed at me about things that had happened almost fifty years ago, I realized my sister was never going to find happiness. She was never going to get past any of the tragedies that had happened in our childhood. She blamed every situation, every bad decision, and every failure on what had happened so long ago. She was not capable of seeing that she had had choices, crossroads, and other paths that she could have taken in her life. Forever, in her head and heart, she would remain that little girl being raped with no one to save her.

The fact that I had seemed to raise myself out of the depths of anguish she was feeling, with the help of a loving husband and two wonderful sons and a slew of therapists and psychiatrists, didn't seem to enter her reality. She was so filled with rage because I had, and she hadn't.

She believed she wasn't responsible for any of the problems, struggles, or decisions in her life. She even yelled that when she refused to do something as simple as clean her house, she was getting back at Daddy for making us clean the house so much as children. I stopped her and said, "Debbie, do you hear yourself? Daddy has been dead for almost thirty years! How does that possibly get back at Daddy?"

While the conversation was heated, we left the room together. She was calm and smiling. I thank God she had been able to unload a lot of her pain.

Three months later, I saw my sister at my nephew's house where we were celebrating his wife's birthday. Debbie came limping down the driveway using a little pink cane. Her eighteen-month-old grandson ran to meet her. She was smiling at him, and he was smiling at her, pulling on her other hand to come with him. He adored his grandma, and

Debbie adored him. She seemed better than she had been in a while. We had a good talk. Little did I know, it would be the last time I would see my Sissy alive.

On June 22, 2015, I got a call at work that Debbie had fallen in the parking lot of her apartment and that I needed to come quickly. While on my way, my niece called me, screaming that her mom was dead.

Debbie probably had a stroke, a blood clot, or a heart attack, due to her atrial fibrillation. We will never know for sure what took her. Whatever it was, she had died alone on the hard concrete. I pray that she didn't know anything, and that it was quick.

Though I had lost my Sissy years before as I rocked under a desk while she cried, I lost her forever that day.

A memorial to Debbie, my Sissy.

Well, Sissy, I have been dreading this all day long. Today, you would have turned 60. We would've all gone to El Nopal's in J-town square and sat at Pedro's table. You would've had a margarita or two. We would've had a great time celebrating your big day.

Sissy, today I ache for you. We had so many differences, but we shared so much of the first 25 years of our lives. We both made it through those early years of terror. You paid for my junior prom dress because I couldn't afford it. You were my maid of honor, as I was yours. You babysat Austin for his first two years, and I was the first to hold your son at his birth. We raised our kids together, to be like brothers and sisters to each other. Holidays and birthdays were always celebrated together.

I am so afraid, being the last one left from our home, that I will forget the stories of our youth. Of sneaking Dinty Moore beef stew in the living room when Daddy was gone on active duty. Of watching Daddy throw giant globs of tinsel on the tree at Christmas, and watching Mom separate the globs when Daddy wasn't watching.

Sissy, I took flowers to your grave today. They were not stargazer lilies, but they were lilies in your favorite color. I hope they bring a smile to your face.

I love you and miss you. Happy birthday in Heaven.

Shannon, August 2, 2018

* * *

Two little girls before life threw any punches. Two little girls who were best friends and loved each other so much. Two little girls, who knew only love. Two little girls who were sugar and spice and everything nice.

On your 62nd birthday, Sissy, I miss who those two little girls could have become together. I miss the love we could have shared, as well as the love we did share.

I miss us.

Most of all, I miss you, my big sister. On your birthday, I pray you are healed, covered in love and at peace.

Happy birthday, my sweet Sissy! I love you!

Shannon, August 2, 2020

* * *

Sissy today is a bit unusual for your birthday. At 2:30 in the afternoon, it is only 78 degrees. It is a beautiful blue-sky day, as I look out on my butterfly garden in full bloom. I am going to cut a bouquet of blossoms to take to your grave today. Hot pink flowers from the crepe myrtles, deep purple blooms from the butterfly bushes, and light pink caps from the hydrangeas.

It seems as if you have been gone forever, and yet, as I type this, I can still hear you laughing at some silly story we share from the past. I feel your breath on my cheek as you tell me some long ago secret. You give me one of your Big Sissy bear hugs, and I feel peace.

I imagine you enjoy watching our kids and grandkids from your place in Heaven. The little ones are growing up so fast. I wonder if you catch all their day-to-day cuteness. I hope so.

On this day, your 63rd birthday, I send you so much love, and I hope you can feel it from so far away.

I love you, Sissy ...

August 2, 2021

* * *

Seven years, Sissy. Seven years plus two days since I last heard your voice. Since I hugged you. Since we laughed together.

I know I will see you again, hear your voice again, hug you again, and we will laugh in the joy of the presence of The Lord. Our tears will be a thing of the past, eternally. Only everlasting joy for us, Sissy.

Shannon, June 22, 2022

Twenty-Two

In this chapter, you will find the pictures documenting our years with Fr. Kevin. I have looked at them hundreds of times, and I still find them shocking in what they represent. They mark the trail of a pedophile at work and play.

On some of them I have been able to identify the dates by what the subject matter is, and others by dates that were written on the back of the pictures. Some had the date printed on them by the photo processing company.

> In going over the pictures, unfortunately, I have also had to come to terms with the fact that some of the memories I had hoped were not really true were. Such was the memory I have always feared that Fr. Kevin had taken us back to his apartment the evening of my First Communion.

After carefully studying the pictures taken that day, April 28, 1968, it is evident that Debbie and I are wearing the same clothes and hair do's in these pictures at our home and at Fr. Kevin's apartment.

It breaks my heart to know what occurred just hours after my Blessed First Holy Communion to both of us.

He really did believe he was God's man. He was again making us God's Brides, and he was showing us God's love.

Shannon's First Communion Day at Her Home

Shannon's First Communion Day at Fr. Kevin's Apartment

There are also pictures he took of us within a short time of Debbie's First Communion in 1966, though probably not on her First Communion Day, due to her wearing a different color of shoes in the picture.

There are a couple of pictures of us at the Shaughnessy home, where my father was born in the upstairs bedroom. There are pictures of us on summer vacations with him, In the backyard with him. At the lake with him. Him at Debbie's birthday party. He. Was. Everywhere.

Pictures of the China plates Dad had painted in Japan from the photographs Fr. Kevin took of us in his apartment are here.

A picture of my First Communion dress with the burn holes from his ashes is here.

There were pictures of all "his girls" however due to respecting of privacy, they are not shared here. How many more of "his girls" were there? How many more are still alive, living with the pain and shame of what he did to us?

Here is a picture of the chapel at the college where he lived, where he celebrated my parents' tenth anniversary mass in November 1967.

Here are some additional photos that I have from my childhood and my time with Fr. Kevin.

Shannon and Debbie in "Their Date" Dresses in Fr. Kevin's Apartment

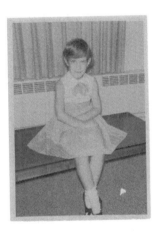

But When I Fly ...

Last week, I was home sick with bronchitis. I went into the basement to try to find some of my books I had packed away before our move. Reading is my passion, so if all you can do when you are sick is rest, reading is the perfect way to rest even when you aren't asleep.

So, the first container I opened had old pictures and letter. They were the ones I saved after Mom's death in 2001. Things I hadn't seen in a very long time. I scooped up a stack of pictures and letters, figuring I could spend some time reading and reminiscing.

I read the letters from my father first. They were from when he was deployed in 1968 and 1969, when I was just shy of eight years old until about my ninth birthday. They were sweet letters, telling me he loved and missed us, and that he was proud of us. He mentioned that when he got home, he would tease me, as we loved to tease each other, and he would also share a few sips of beer with me.

Next, I found the letters from Fr. Kevin while he was deployed. If you didn't know it, you probably wouldn't catch the little things he mentioned that hint at what he liked to do with his "favorite girls." In one letter, he included a picture of his desktop. It was covered with pictures. Pictures of "his girls." Debbie's and my pictures were center stage. All the pictures were of little girls. All of them. I don't know who the others were, but I weep and pray for them.

As a survivor, and most of the time a thriver, I still have so many confusing thoughts and feelings about those years when Fr. Kevin was around us. I often play a question-and-answer game in my head, Why did you let him do those horrible things to you and not tell anyone for so long? Why did you write him letters? Why did you like getting postcards and letters from your abuser? Does that make you complicit?

And then I go back to all the years in therapy spent trying to come to terms with my past. All the support, knowledge, compassion, empathy and realism given to me by my therapists Martha, Craig, and Anne, as well as my psychiatrist.

When you are four years old, you many times don't know, nor understand, what is appropriate behavior for adults. You do what you are told. You trust your parents, and those they allow in your everyday life.

Then, when the pedophile has you, there are always ways to keep you in line. Mommy and Daddy said you must always do whatever Fr. Kevin tells you to do. And he's a priest. God's man. Everyone does what the priest says to do.

When the physical pain comes, yet more things are told to you. You are special. Only very special little girls get to have God's love from God's man. See how very special you are?

When that doesn't work anymore, the threats start. You can't EVER talk about our special God's love time. If you do, I will hurt Sissy. I will hurt your mommy or your daddy. Besides, no one will believe you anyway. You're just a kid. I am an adult, and a priest.

And so, you survive. You survive any way you can. You go to your secret place in your head. You fly far, far away while he's doing those terrible, awful, painful things. You no longer let yourself think about why.

Years later, you finally realize you did the best you could have done. And that, on your weak days, you still just survive; you just get through it,

But on those strong days, you do more. You truly thrive. You REALLY fly! And the one true God sends his angels to fly with you!!

Shannon, 2018

Twenty-Three

With the loss of my Sissy, I realized a life-long road of healing would be necessary if I wanted to live a fully engaged life. I felt I needed to become more aware of the good and gracious deeds God had done for me that gave my life meaning and value.

On this journey of healing, God always put people in my life to help me heal. Sometimes it is obvious the person is a part of the healing process, such as my therapists, friends and some in clergy positions. Others have helped in ways I could never fathom, with the perfect words or gestures at just the right moment. Many I didn't recognize for days, months or even years. Sometimes, the healing itself brought at first great pain but then led to a new way of thinking, feeling and living. These next pages are in remembrance of those who gave of themselves, sometimes causing themselves pain, to heal the brokenness in me.

Sometimes, God chooses those who seem totally unable to fit into the healing process. Such is the first person who dared to step out of his comfort zone simply to aid me in healing.

In 2002 when Debbie and I entered the lawsuit against the Archdiocese of Louisville, the person I talked to on the phone identified himself as Brian. I mistakenly believed he was the Chancellor of the Archdiocese, Dr. Brian Reynolds, but he wasn't. This Brian was a deacon who was fielding the vast number of calls coming into the archdiocese concerning sexual abuse.

In 2002 and for the next year or so, the archbishop at the time, Thomas Kelly, and Dr. Reynolds, the Chancellor of the Archdiocese, represented the Church on an almost daily basis in the local media. It was anything but pretty. Our lawyers were able to secure thousands of documents showing how deep the cover up of the sexual abuse of minors had been for decades in our archdiocese.

The more I heard and read, the worse my pain and depression became. In most of the stories, Dr. Reynolds was the spokesperson, which made him even more the arch enemy, if you will, to me. I felt such animosity towards both men. The lawsuit was finally settled in June 2003, and the awards were dispersed in late 2003 to early 2004.

IN THE SUMMER OF 2005, MY PASTOR, FR. SCOTT WIMSETT, CALLED ME.

He told me Dr. Reynolds had called him and asked him to set up a meeting for himself, me, and Steve, with Fr. Scott facilitating. Dr. Reynolds understood my anger over my abuse, but he didn't understand why I was so angry specifically with him. Dr. Reynolds wanted to know what he could do to help me to heal and wanted to start by addressing the great anger I had against him. After a lot of discussion and prayer, I decided to meet with Dr. Reynolds.

On the afternoon we met, we all went into the room, and I don't know who was more nervous. We all had so much to lose, but we also had so much to gain if we only gave each other a chance. I quickly learned that some days, the true presence of the Holy Spirit can change the path of your life in short order.

Dr. Reynolds told me he was there to listen to anything I needed to say. He decided my healing was more important than his comfort level. He very humbly listened for hours. He offered no reasons, no excuses, and no comments unless I asked him a specific question.

And a new type of healing started that day. Because, as Fr. Scott told me, those moments were holy. What happened that day was holy.

In the years since that day, Brian—as I now call him since I consider him a friend—has been a staunch support for me and my now-deacon husband. He is never more than a phone call away if I need to talk with him. He continues to help me walk through the minefield of recovery from abuse.

I have learned that if you want to change anything in your life, you must also understand that other people may not be who you have made them to be in your mind. So many times, we put people in these boxes of who we think they are without giving them a chance to be who they really are.

I wasted years of my life in anger over what had happened. But by taking a chance in meeting with Brian, I was able to let another burden that was not mine to carry fall to the ground.

I pray that you, the reader, can find a few nuggets of holiness and wisdom of what not to do to heal, as much as what to do on your healing journey. Sometimes, I've held on to memories and pain that I should have let go decades ago, simply because I didn't know who I would be without them.

Come home to Jesus.
His yoke is easy, and His burden is light.

Shannon, undated

Twenty-Four

I am one who is usually very resistant to change, but considering how I felt about Archbishop Kelly, I was relieved when his tenure as archbishop was concluded.

As mandated by the Vatican rules, he sent his letter of resignation to the Pope on the occasion of his seventy-fifth birthday.

IN 2007, WE GOT A NEW SHEPHERD, AND FOR ME, A NEW WAY TO TRUST.

Archbishop Joseph Kurtz was installed as the new archbishop of Louisville. I first saw him at the groundbreaking ceremony for our new church building in 2008. Steve and I met him personally when Steve was accepted into the diaconate formation program in 2011.

Over the next five years, we had the honor of being with our Archbishop on many occasions. Since Steve's ordination in 2016, that has continued.

Anyone who meets Archbishop Kurtz knows he is a people person. He meets you and never forgets your name. He is the most personable person I believe I have ever met. He is a man committed to being a shepherd to his people.

Archbishop Kurtz met with me on multiple occasions to help me with healing from my abuse. He was always compassionate and respectful. It was very evident that abuse such as mine causes him great pain and distress, as a person, as a priest and as a shepherd.

I truly believe he would, if he could, move mountains to take away my past abuse. His kindness, patience and prayers have brought me comfort. With thousands of people under his care, I am very grateful for his thoughtful guidance, fervent prayers and gentleness.

He has helped me to learn, as well as believe, that trust of clergy and hierarchy can and is possible.

Early one morning, after attending mass at the church next to the chancellery office, I met with Archbishop Kurtz concerning helpful programs for survivors of abuse. Deacon Pat was with me for support because Steve couldn't get away from work.

I asked the archbishop if I could bring an empty chair over to sit beside me, to remind me that the Holy Spirit was in the room with us. He smiled and said of course.

I don't think people realize how blessed we are to have a shepherd to lead us who is gentle and yet exuberant, genuine, and kind, and aware of the needs of others. He must have known that I would probably be nervous and uncomfortable because he set such a comforting tone for the meeting.

This reminds me of one of the major things we learned during formation -- Meet people where they are. Walk with them, not in front of or behind. Get down in the muck with them. Go the distance with them. Let them know you are not going to run away if they show you the horrible, ugly, and deep wounds they bring with them.

So, the next time you get the chance, walk with the wounded. Talk with the inmate. Listen to a dying friend. Hold the hand of the addict. Get down in the muck and sit with them awhile. You will come out of it with new perspectives and a renewed hope in man.

Shannon, 2023

Twenty-Five

T he next person on the list of helpers is a gentleman I met at a convention in downtown Louisville during the aftermath of the lawsuit. There were several speakers talking about clergy sexual abuse. I remember only bits and pieces of that day. I believe it was in 2003 or 2004. I know I got up and spoke for a few short minutes and then had to leave because I was so overwhelmed. This very genteel older man standing in the hallway said hello. I acknowledged him and left to go home.

Soon after, I was asked to attend a meeting of a new survivor's support group in Louisville, called Voice of the. Faithful. And there was that same genteel man! This time, I remembered his name from our brief introduction—Vince Grenough. He oversaw this newly formed group.

I was bringing in a video that chronicled abuse victim stories. I had shared my story in the video and thought I was just dropping it off. Vince was under the impression I was going to introduce it, watch it and lead a discussion. At that point, I had never even seen the whole video myself. Needless to say, it was a very hard night. Vince, a retired therapist, must have seen my turmoil and pulled me through the evening with grace and love.

From that night on, Vince became the first man who had ever showed me by his words and actions how a man could emulate the vocation of fatherhood faithfully and safely. He made me feel heard, safe, and loved in an appropriate way. He was patient, kind, and thoughtful in every circumstance.

Finally, I had person who I felt safe using a name with the connation of a father. But he couldn't be Dad, Daddy, or Father. Those words were too triggering. My soul felt I needed to honor Vince's place in my life with a name that showed the importance of our relationship. And so, after years of therapy and healing, I felt strong enough to use a word for a father figure, one which I had never used before.

In that moment, I chose to call Vince my beloved Papa.

Papa has seen me through some of the best and worst times of my life since that night. Papa has become one of my most trusted sounding boards. He always points me to true north. He has the gentlest soul of anyone I have ever known in my whole life. He has the sweetest laugh and the warmest hugs. He calms the storms in my head with the smooth tone of voice that I am sure helped hundreds in his years as a therapist.

I traveled to Nicaragua on a mission trip with Papa in 2005 to help in some of the worst poverty I have ever seen. We worked for a week with children and adults, painting, building, and feeding those we met. Every day, the temperature was over one hundred degrees, and there was no air conditioning. And there was seventy-four-year-old Papa, always smiling, working, and telling another story or listening to someone else's story.

Steve and I visit Papa and his love, Pat, every time we get a chance, as they live hundreds of miles away now. I truly feel I have found my way home when I see his sweet face.

Today, I had to go back to the neighborhood and church where I grew up. One of my oldest and dearest friends from childhood lost her mother. I did the best I could to prepare myself for all the old triggers.

Most of the people I knew from the area have either died or moved somewhere else in the forty years since I left as a new bride. I did see and talk to six of the parishioners I still knew. Of course, because the original church burned down in 1997, at least I didn't have to go into the same physical building that was the site of so much terror for Sissy and me.

Driving down the streets past my many friends' houses brought to mind children running to and from different houses so long ago. Going past the softball field where I played, and my father coached made it seem like it all had happened yesterday. Seeing my childhood home made me think how normal that house of horror looked.

The celebration of the funeral mass was well attended, as this wonderful lady had a large family and was also one of the founding members of the parish. You could feel the love for her and the blessings of the faith she had shared with so many throughout her life.

I thought I had done amazingly well, until I got to my car to leave. Out of nowhere, I was hit with nausea so bad I thought I would surely throw up in my car. I tried slow, deep breathing. I tried praying. Finally, I picked up my phone and called Papa.

Papa answered and I told him where I was and what was happening. He very calmly talked with me. He helped me to push the terror away and rejoin the year 2022, where I was an adult not a child in the midst of abuse. When we agreed that I was in a better frame of mind, we hung up and I started on my way home.

Papa is now ninety years old. Reality tells me my beloved Papa isn't going to be here forever to help me. But on days like today, how I thank God, and Papa, that he is here now.

Shannon, April 30, 2022

Twenty-Six

A nother person I will classify as one of my healers is going to be fun. I adore the way he uses humor to engage people everywhere he goes. This priest often starts his homilies off each weekend by walking in front of the altar with a quirky little grin on his face, making you wonder what he is about to say. I remember him telling me I should be careful what I told him because anything could make good homily material!

THE FIRST TIME STEVE AND I MET FR. SCOTT WIMSETT IN THE FALL OF 2003, HE SAT US IN FRONT OF THE WINDOW.

He had the office door open and a large desk between him and me. He later told me he was a little worried about meeting the woman who wrote the editorial in the *Courier Journal* about then-Archbishop Kelly, which had been printed just four months before. We were there because we had moved into the parish and wanted to get registered. I still needed the one thing no other church could offer: the Holy Eucharist. I think God himself put us in Fr. Scott's office to bring me back to church. Fr.

Scott was able to make us feel welcomed at this little parish in the country.

Fr. Scott helped me sort through the theology of how to deal with my feelings. I had—and to some extent still have—so much guilt over not being able to think of God and Jesus the way most people do. Fr. Scott would listen to me in my anguish and try to help me make sense of it. Many times, he would break it down in a way in which I could finally just let go. How many times I heard him say after telling him something, "Well, Shannon, have you thought about it this way?"

In August 2009, I had an injury at work and for a month was in extreme pain. As always, when I am super stressed and can't sleep, whether due to emotional or physical pain, I began having more problems than usual with PTSD and dissociation.

On September 21, 2009, I had a major dissociative break and attempted suicide. Because of the quick reactions and response of several people, I was rushed to the hospital. I was given IV Narcan in the ambulance and at some point, though I don't remember it, was given some type of charcoal solution to drink.

A few hours later, while I was still in the emergency room, Fr. Scott came in. I smiled at him, and he busted out laughing. I didn't know my teeth were black due to the charcoal. He told me I should know that wasn't a good look for me.

Fr. Scott was moved to another parish in 2011. We still talk when our schedules allow, but we both know we are each but a phone call or text away.

Lord, help me to remember to look to you in both my pain and my joy.

So often, I get so caught up in the moment I am in that I forget you are always there with me. Thank you for always putting strong and compassionate people on my journey's path. Each person is a walking prayer sent at the perfect time by you to show me how involved you are in my healing.

And thank you for continuing to send my road map to me through others when I am too weak to even know there is a road. Oh, what a beautiful journey we are traveling together!

Shannon, July 2022

Twenty-Seven

In 2009, Steve came to me and told me he felt he had a calling to be a deacon. Knowing that the wife had to go through all the formation classes with her spouse, my first response was a very emphatic, *"Hell NO!!"* We had many arguments about this for a few weeks or months. Steve told me I was being selfish, and I was astonished at his insensitivity. I refused to consider it and knowing that the wife had to sign off on it before he could apply, Steve gave it up.

IN 2011, STEVE AGAIN APPROACHED THE SUBJECT OF THE DIACONATE.

I again said no. He pleaded with me, telling me again of his deep yearning and calling for the diaconate. Finally on a Sunday afternoon, we went to an information meeting on the diaconate. I cringed sitting in a room with all these guys in clerical collars. But as I watched my husband, I could see that yearning in his eyes.

Steve, with my blessing, applied for the deacon formation program the next day. He was accepted into the class of 2016.

When Steve applied to become a deacon in the Archdiocese of Louisville, neither one of us had any clue just how much our lives were about to change. Upon entering formation in July 2011, we met nineteen other couples, our two sponsor couples, and the deacon director and his wife who would all journey through the five years of discernment and formation with us. This group of people became our closest friends and lifeline.

We are one of the most diverse groups of people you could put together in one room. The youngest were in their thirties and the oldest approaching sixty. Some already had grandchildren, and one couple had just gotten married. Another couple had their first child while in formation. Some had only a high school diploma while one had a PhD. We had retired military. We had strict conservatives and staunch liberals. We had wine connoisseurs and NASCAR fans. We had three schoolteachers, three nurses, and a mammographer. And we had a room chock full of people who wanted to learn how to use their God given talents to serve their Lord in the best ways they could.

At our third discernment Saturday in the fall of 2011, Steve and I shared my story with the permission of the deacon director. We felt we needed to be upfront about my past, as we knew parts of our classes had the probability of triggering my PTSD. We also let Dr. Brian Reynolds know what we were going to do, and he decided he would be there so he could follow up with answers to our classmates to any questions they might have involving policy and procedures of the archdiocese in respect to the handling of child sexual abuse.

I remember little of that day. Somewhere, Steve has saved what he and I read to our classmates. I remember being cold, and I think I may have cried. I know afterwards, I laid on a couch in the lobby with one of our sponsor couple wives until Steve came out, and then he and I went home.

From that day forward, our classmates became a solid wall of support for Steve and me.

Formation for me, was wonderful and awful, holy, and terribly triggering. When different topics were covered that triggered wounds and I left the room, there was always someone, or in many cases, several people who would come sit with me, talk with me, or walk with me.

They held me when I cried.
They dried my tears and listened to my anger.
They gave me hope that we could get through this hour, this day, this year, this formation, and this life.

They were, and still are, the most faithful and faith-filled people I have ever known. Steve and I would not have made it through the five years of formation without their ever-present support and prayers.

Though I know theologically humans can never become angels, our classmates felt like a room full of what I believe are representative of how guardian angels are supposed to be. They watched over me, guided me, and protected me. We will forever be grateful to the Class of 2016 for the multitude of selfless gifts they bestowed on us.

A few days ago, while talking with some close deacon couple friends, the subject of guardian angels came up. I recalled that last year, I went to pick our grandchildren up from religious education class at church and heard them reciting a prayer I didn't recall hearing before. It went like this:

*Angel of God, my
guardian dear, to
whom God's love
commits me here,
ever this day be at
my side, to light,
to guard, to rule,
and guide.
Amen*

The children sounded so sweet saying this prayer, but I have, since 1992, felt very torn about guardian angels. You see, Fr. Kevin's gift to me for my First Holy Communion in 1968, on the day before my eighth birthday, was the classic picture of two small children crossing over a bridge with their guardian angel hovering above them for protection. That picture hung over my bed from that day until the day I got married in 1982. Yes, it hung there at the same time Fr. Kevin gave me baths so Mom could relax, and then he said prayers over me and "tucked me into bed" for years. I stared at that picture that was supposed to show my guardian angel protecting me as he abused me.

I wonder if that ever entered Fr. Kevin's mind when he was doing it? Did he even realize he was who my guardian angel was supposed to be keeping away from me?

And so, I have a choice. I can choose to stay in that bedroom with those memories, or I can choose to take the hand of my guardian angel and walk out of that room forever. Those are the days of my past that I will leave behind. Today, I choose to take her hand and fly with her to the new days of my life.

Shannon, undated

Twenty-Eight

Most people have nasty, sarcastic jokes about lawyers. I am one of the lucky ones who has been blessed with only positive encounters with lawyers. But even among good lawyers, I must mention one who represents what a lawyer is supposed to be about.

In my mind, a lawyer is supposed to be a servant too. He or she is supposed to represent their client to the best of their ability and win justice for them. They should never lose sight of who and what they are fighting for.

In a meeting in 2002 or 2003 at my attorney's office, a few of us survivors were seated around a large table in the conference room. Several were telling their stories to the group. After hearing just a few, I fled the room.

I ran out of the conference room and into a small kitchen/break room. I found a small corner, got down in that corner, and started rocking. Debbie had followed me and got down on the floor with me. She knew that I had dissociated, and she would just have to wait it out with me.

The youngest attorney in the firm, Hans Poppe, came in, and seeing me scrunched up and rocking in the corner, got right down on the floor with Debbie and me and stayed right there with us. He didn't try to get me up or move me. He just stayed with us, right where we were. He talked calmly and soothingly, according to Debbie. He guarded us from anyone else coming into the kitchen area.

In the years since then, Hans and his assistant, Barbara Crawford, have been staunch supporters of both Debbie and me and have been available whenever we have called them.

Hans is one of the top attorneys in the commonwealth of Kentucky, and in my opinion, he is the best attorney in Kentucky. Hans and Barbara still check up on me, twenty years after we first met. Hans is one kick-ass lawyer, but he is also a tenderhearted servant of the people he represents.

Barbara is the matriarch that keeps everyone towing the line at the Poppe Law Firm. She is also one of the warmest and kindest people I have ever known. And they are both a blessing to all who know them. God bless them for all those they have helped!

I asked Hans to write about the lawsuit from his view as one of our attorneys. I think it's important to understand what that whole process looked like, as well as to show the energy Hans and the other attorneys brought to our legal team. Hans graciously put this together to give you a better view into our case, and what we were fighting for.

Most everyone has heard of The Catholic Archdiocese of Boston childhood sexual abuse scandal and settlement. There's even a Wikipedia page about it. But what you probably haven't heard about is the settlement with The Roman Catholic Archdiocese of Louisville for $25.7 million dollars that preceded, and may have contributed to, the Boston settlement about six months later. The cases were equally important, and the victims equally scarred.

Louisville, Kentucky has a population of about 600,000, of which 200,000 are Catholics. And it was also home to a single priest the New York Times referred to as "what may be the worst serial abuser among the priests who have been called to account anywhere in the nation."

The scandal broke from a single phone call to the law firm I was working at in 2002. A man, then forty-five, had read an article about a priest being forced to retire due to abuse allegations. He had not forgotten the priest, or what the priest did to him. He contacted us and told us he had been abused as a child by the retiring priest. And he said there were others. Lots of others. We filed suit against The. Archdiocese on his behalf. Our phones began ringing.

Scared and hurt, people slowly began revealing their secrets. They had been abused by thirty-eight priests, brothers, and other church employees of The Archdiocese. One by one they came forward at first. This heavily catholic community was skeptical of our claims. Some were indignant that the abuse didn't happen.

Some called the victims frauds and liars. And those were the nice things. The Louisville community was deeply fractured by the claims being made. But eventually, doctors, lawyers, and accountants came forward to file suits. And when a local celebrity came forward and filed suit, the floodgates opened.

Suits were filed in batches of twenty-five-plus at a time. Eventually we filed suit on behalf of 243 victims of childhood sexual abuse (The 243.) Louisville was the nation's only jurisdiction in which every single plaintiff sued by name, rather than as John or Jane doe, or by their initials. This was crucial in building credibility in the community that these allegations were true and serious.

Some victims were still struggling with the trauma from the abuse, others had been able to lead relatively normal lives, others were retraumatized by coming forward publicly. But all shared one thing in common. They were betrayed by the very institution that should have protected them from these monsters. The Church not only failed, but it also facilitated the abuse by concealing allegations of abuse, by moving "problem" priests from parish to parish, and by keeping secret Canon 489 files that supported allegations of abuse. The Church was an accomplice to the crimes with its "geographic solution" to the problem and failure to comply with its legal obligation to report to authorities.

Eventually, many of these priests would admit to their crimes and admit to The Archdiocese failing to take any action. The priests who weren't already dead went to prison. The Archdiocese acted worse than any other corporate defendant in history. No other institution could have survived a scandal of this magnitude.

Fourteen months after filing the first lawsuit, all 243 victims reached a settlement with The Archdiocese for what was then the largest settlement ever paid directly from the assets of a diocese, $25.7 million dollars—half the church's cash assets. And the settlement agreement included one other thing. An agreement in writing that The Archdiocese would never again refer to The 243 as "alleged" victims.

In a way, Louisville's story is unique. In a way it is not. Childhood sexual abuse has been a problem within The Catholic Church for decades, if not centuries. And it has been dealt with substantially similar all over the world. But in Louisville, where one third of the citizens are catholic, the sheer magnitude of abuse was staggering. The 243 came forward. We will never know how many more there were, but I suspect it's in the hundreds based on the number of supportive phone calls we received from people saying they were also abused but would not come forward for personal reasons.

I am proud to have represented The 243. Those brave souls willing to take a public stand against one of the wealthiest and richest institutions in the world, The Catholic Church. Their courage forced The Church to take financial and public accountability and to offer pastoral and other counseling for anyone abused by the hands of clergy or other employees. It forced the Church to make policy changes to deal with allegations of abuse differently and to believe victims who were abused.

And chief among those leading the charge for change and reform was Shannon Shaughnessy Age. May we all persevere to overcome our pain and channel it for positive change the way she did.

Supreme Court Justice Louis D. Brandeis, from Louisville, was fond of saying "Sunshine is the best disinfectant." Shannon, and the rest of The 243, brought a boat load of sunshine to The Archdiocese of Louisville. Sunshine that spread across the country and emboldened other victims in other diocese to come forward and demand accountability. The braveness of The 243 in publicly coming forward reverberated in dioceses across the country. And, for that, we owe them a debt of gratitude.

I wish The 243 peace, comfort, and healing as they move forward in this life. I wish you, the reader, the same.

Hans. G. Poppe
Attorney for The 243

Twenty-Nine

In July 2018, hundreds of clergy abuse cases broke in Pennsylvania and elsewhere in the US. All the sudden, clergy abuse was on the front page again. As you might imagine, it was brutal waking up to these reports daily.

IN SEPTEMBER 2018, WE ATTENDED OUR ARCHDIOCESE'S DEACON ASSEMBLY DAY.

I gave a short talk about the newest crisis in the church. Steve and I had unique gifts in these trying times. We are a deacon couple who has lived through the aftermath of abuse, and we are called to serve the broken-hearted in the world, especially in this diocese and in our parish.

I made a plea to the assembly, telling them we need to walk with those who have suffered abuse and their families in a concrete and tangible way. As a survivor, my experience of going through another crisis publicly for the second time, saying "I'm sorry" is not enough. I believe it is imperative, as deacon couples, that we should personally reach out to survivors and just *be* with them. Listen. Let them tell you of the pain, the anger, the shame, and the hopelessness that is a part of them. I know it's not easy to hear, but as we were all taught in formation, it's necessary if we are to be God's hands doing His holy work.

I then told them of a weeklong retreat program which began in the United States in 2005. Dr. Theresa Burke composed the retreat entitled called Grief to Grace—Healing the Wounds of Abuse. Dr. Burke was invited to provide an overview of this sensory based treatment which integrates spiritual, psychological, and somatic awareness in 2007 for the ISCB National Victim Assistance. In September, Coordinator meeting. This program was first presented in 2007 at the National Victim Assistance Coordinator meeting. She also taught about effective approaches for Trauma Informed Care. Since then, many dioceses have covered the cost of the retreat for clergy abuse victims as the program continues to spread throughout the world. It has expanded to seventeen countries and six languages, with other translations in progress.

Pope Francis has personally endorsed Grief to Grace. *"These are fruitful works, which heal, which pour out mercy."* Many other bishops have attended the program and given strong endorsements. In 2018, the Pope's anti abuse committee met with Fr. Dominic Allain, who serves as the international Pastoral Director of Grief to Grace at a meeting in London.

Bishop Thomas Olmsted of the Phoenix diocese has said, "Those who have suffered abuse need to experience the loving and healing ministry of the Church. This can be particularly true when a person has been abused by a representative of the Church in the past."

Dr. Theresa Burke, the founder, said, "No one had been talking about healing or how people can help victims besides extending statutes of limitations, and more lawsuits, panels, and investigations along with ongoing apologies as the scope of abuse in the church continues to broaden. Victims **DO** want someone to address the shattering spiritual injuries of the abuse."

Now, there was a man in the audience who was a deacon candidate in formation. He took the information back to his pastor, Fr. Ben Cameron of the Fathers of Mercy. Fr. Ben just happens to be very good friends with Dr. Theresa Burke, founder of Grief to Grace and Rachel's Vineyard, the program for women who have had abortions.

Soon we met Fr. Ben for dinner and realized we all wanted to attend a Grief to Grace retreat and investigate the possibility of bringing this type of retreat to the Louisville area.

NEXT, I SET UP A MEETING WITH ARCHBISHOP KURTZ.

As always, our Archbishop was firmly behind anything that might help healing victims of abuse. But this program was also for anyone who suffered abuse, not just clergy sexual abuse. This program could help so many people within not just our archdiocese, but also in our region of the US.

After much discussion, the archdiocese decided to investigate Grief to Grace by sending Steve and me to a retreat. Fr. Ben also obtained a sponsor to go as well. We filled out the applications and were scheduled to go in February 2019. But a blizzard kept us from making it.

We rescheduled our attendance to a retreat for September 2019 in New Jersey.

It was life changing. It is a very much Christ-centered approach to healing but in ways I never imagined.

It was hard work, as anything worth doing is, but the benefits are real and tangible. I would recommend this program to anyone!

Because COVID-19 came so quickly on the heels of our return from the retreat, and with it the shutting down of so much in our country, we had to put our plans for Grief to Grace on hold. We are hopeful that God will show us how to proceed in the future.

With the closeness retreats bring to retreatants, of course, Steve, Fr. Ben, and I came away with a deeper friendship. Fr. Ben met Little Shannon at the retreat, and he also saw me finally be able to let go of a lot of that pent-up anger. He knows the good, bad, and ugly of those early years, and he didn't run away when I told him all about it. He may have shed a few tears, he may have been angry at what had happened, but he did not run. That is a blessing.

Fr. Ben has a passionate calling to walk with hurting people, and he has walked figuratively many miles with me. Sometimes we talk, sometimes we look at the scenery; at the beauty God has put around us, and sometimes we just walk silently, without words, because no words can cover the pain. And in that silence, in the quiet, I find God.

For many years, I couldn't figure out why so much of my life's work put me in direct contact with priests.

I worked for many years with a priest in Appalachia in our mission work. I have been involved in many programs and positions at our parishes that required me to be in close proximity and contact with priests. At times, I felt God had a pretty cruel sense of humor. If God really loved me, why did I keep needing to work directly with a man wearing a collar to do what God was seemingly leading and calling me to?

I now believe God led me to all these endeavors to show that I didn't need to fear everyone who wears a collar.

He showed me so many good, holy priests who were and are dedicated to their vows as priests. He made me see that, although Fr. Kevin showed me the depths of the worst kind of priest, he was the exception, not the rule. He also knew that one day, my own husband would wear a collar as a deacon.

As painful as it was for years, I now thank God for working this out for me exactly as He did.

Shannon, July 2022

Thirty

A few years ago, Steve and I were asked to be on a panel discussion group at a local church to talk about clergy sexual abuse. There had recently been a huge number of cases reported nationally, and the subject was once again front-page news. On this panel was the archdiocese contact person for clergy sexual abuse, a psychologist who also was in formation to be a deacon, two licensed therapists, Steve, and myself. I am going to share parts of the reflection I read that night.

* * *

Mary Queen of Peace
Hope & Healing Reflection

Abuse is a lifelong ordeal. Abuse comes to us in many different forms and affects each of us in different ways. Some injuries leave permanent, visible scars, some we barely remember, and some change our lives forever.

As with most major injuries, clergy sexual abuse causes a ripple effect. It not only affects the person abused, but also the victim's family, close friends, and the perpetrator and his family. It affects spirituality, the ability to build relationships, sexuality, intimacy, and the ability to trust oneself and others. With clergy abuse, the ripples spread even further. Because of my friendships with many priests and deacons through the years, I watched many who were deeply wounded and affected in the first round of the abuse scandal in the early 2000's. That aspect became personal to us though when Steve became a member of the clergy and rude comments were directed at us about the Catholic clergy. My heart breaks for all our wonderful faithful clergy who have been so grievously hurt by this scandal.

It's been fifty-five years since my abuse began. I can tell you the effects are still present. My parents, my sister, and Fr. Kevin are now all deceased. I alone am here to sift through the story and find my way. The road to healing has been up and down, twisted and curving, long and hard. It has not been linear. Healing rarely is. For every person on the road to healing, the journey is different. We have lost many on this road to despair, addictions, and death.

Many years ago, one of my therapists who knew that I loved gardening suggested that I use that love of nature to help me in my healing journey. The plan was for me to, in my mind, go out to my garden and work to pull all the horrible memories of the abuse out so that I would be left with only the beautiful flowers in my garden. Kind of a Weed B Gone approach if you will.

That night, in my dreams, I went out to pull the weeds. I pulled weeds for what seemed like hours. When I finally pulled the last weed, I turned around to look back on my accomplishment. What I found, however, was an empty mud pit without a single growing thing in it.

A few weeks ago, we heard in the Gospel about the fig tree that refused to produce fruit. The gardener begged the master to give him one more year to cultivate it, to fertilize it before he had to tear it down. Perhaps by putting manure deeply into the root system around the tree, the tree could produce fruit.

I have thought about this quite a bit these last few weeks. Those of us who have been abused by anybody know about manure. We have stood in it. We have smelled it. Perhaps those who have used it as fertilizer have gone on to grow beautiful flowers in their lives. A good marriage. Gainful employment. Children who are not too messed up. A sense of peace that they are where they are supposed to be at this time in their life.

And perhaps those who only saw the manure as manure are still just smelling its putrid odor in their bitterness in life. They are still stuck in cycles of anger, resentment, envy, greed, addiction, anguish, and pain.

Jesus understands our pain and anguish. You need to look no further than the Garden of Gethsemane to know this. The One who took on all sin had a choice in whether he would take on that sin. He alone knew the awful burden it would be. And with full knowledge, He chose to bear it for you and me.

One of the hardest aspects of our abuse is the fact that it was centered ritualistically on our Catholic faith. Father immersed the abuse with his "theology," if you will, as he was a professor of theology. He especially focused on the sacraments. Because of this, spirituality has been at times very difficult, if not almost impossible. However, for me, I always come back to the Eucharist. Without the Eucharist, I am lost, a ship without a rudder. I have indeed at times tried to leave the Church, but every time, I come running back for My God at His Holy Table for the Eucharist.

I believe two principles have made it possible for me to rise from the abuse I suffered. The first principle is forgiveness. In my heart, I believe that if God is to forgive me all my sins, I must forgive *every* sin made against me. Not just the little ones, or the easy ones, but every single one!

Forgiveness doesn't depend on the mind of the one who hurt you. It doesn't matter if they care, if they are sorry, or if they even know they hurt you. Forgiveness requires the action of only one party—me. Even if reconciliation with my abuser is not possible, I can still choose to forgive. As St. Thomas Aquinas said, *"Nothing so likens you to God as to forgive him who has injured you."*

The second principle is that every human being must be treated with dignity and integrity, simply because he or she is made in the image and likeness of God.

No matter what a person has done, that person was created by God and is loved just as dearly by God as I am. Now, don't go down the road of, oh my goodness, but, look what he did to you! We *all* do things every day to separate us from God's will! And yet, the Great I Am still loves us completely, because God can't do any less! He *is* love!

I believe that, if even only in the last milliseconds of life, a person repents of his sins and asks God's forgiveness, he will spend eternity with God.

In November 2017, Steve and I led a group of our parishioners on a tour of Italy. We hit most of the Catholic history spots. I dreaded going to one location more than the rest, because of its personal meaning to me. My abuser was a Franciscan, and we were to visit Assisi. The monks there would be wearing the same robes Father used to wear. It would be triggering, and the people we were going with did not know my story.

The day arrived for our trip there. We went through the town of

Assisi and then up to the Hermitage and Oratory where St. Francis spent many years. We walked down the narrow, gravel service road and through the gate to this quiet area steeped in history. My fight or flight instinct was on high alert, DEFCON 1 as we walked into the courtyard. We went into the hewn-rock quarters where St. Francis ate, slept, prayed and worked. The quarters were very small, cold and tight.

Along the way, I lost contact with Steve. At last, I exited onto a garden path in the woods where St. Francis and his monks used to walk and pray centuries ago. It was quiet and serene and empty. No one else was around. No one. I was completely alone in the woods, in this place that terrified me. I walked up and down the path and could not see another human soul anywhere. I went back where I had exited the living quarters, but it had an exit-only sign above the door. I searched for another way back but couldn't find one.

I began to panic and cry. Finally, after what seemed like hours but was probably no more than a few minutes, one of my friends came walking back up one of the paths. He saw how upset I was and asked what was wrong. In a very small voice, I explained that I could not find anyone and was terrified. Sensing my panic, he tried to calm me down and assured me he would find a way back for us. I told him we couldn't go back the way we had come because of the exit-only sign.

After searching for a few minutes for another way back, and finding none, he assured me that it was okay to go back the way we had come in.

Upon reentering the courtyard, there stood a monk in monk robes. He greeted us and hugged me. At once, he stood back and said, "I am so sorry I touched you." He spoke with my friend for a few minutes, and we started to make our way out through the entrance gates. The monk once again said, "I am so sorry I touched you." He gave us a blessing, and we left.

As we headed to our bus, I saw Steve. At the same time, I heard a voice behind me softly yell, "Ma'am, please come back, I must talk to you." I thought, Hell no! But then again, the voice said, "Ma'am, please come back, I must talk to you!" I turned, and there stood the monk. I went back.

When I got through the gates, the monk said, *"Please come to my office with me. I have something for you."* I broke down, started ugly crying, and told him my story. He listened, with sorrow in his eyes. He again said, *"I am so sorry I touched you!"* He then gave me a rosary and blessed it. He told me he was so sorry for what had been done to me and my sister.

When I got back to the gravel road, Steve was waiting for me. He could tell I was very upset and shaken by the whole thing. He asked me to tell him what had happened. So I told my sweet deacon, and he listened.

Steve asked me at the end of my telling if I understood what had just happened. I looked at him, trying to figure out where he was going with this. Finally, he said, "Do you remember the gospel where Jesus is waiting on the sand by the sea, cooking fish in a fire as the disciples are coming in from a long night of fishing? Peter recognizes Jesus and jumps out of the boat to reach him. When he reaches Jesus, Jesus asks Peter three times, do you love me? Peter answers three times, Lord you know I do! Peter had denied Jesus three times, so Peter had to say he loved Jesus three times. And now this monk at Assisi, who has never seen you before and didn't know your story tells you he's sorry he touched you three times. Perhaps, Jesus is teaching us about forgiveness again, and Father Kevin did repent and ask God for forgiveness. Perhaps he is now in purgatory. And perhaps, through a monk at Assisi, he just told you he is so sorry for touching you!"

Perhaps we *all* need to realize that Jesus came to heal us all. From every pain, every affliction, and every sin. All we must do is ask. Because God wants every single one of his prodigal sons and daughters home with him for eternity, no matter how great or small their sin. If he who *is* love wanted anything but all, he wouldn't be the Great I Am!!

Race, race, race away time,
Fly past like the raging wind.
Leave behind a whispered memory,
Of times past and fantasies of then.
Roar like a lion and peak like a mountain,
With all your dreams to come true.
Shine like a star, and glow like a candle
For a future that's bright and new.

Shannon, June, 12, 1981

Epilogue

It has taken years of talking about writing this book, while praying for the courage, the strength, and the wisdom to be true to my family and fair to both the Church and all those involved. I believe I have done that. I feel a sense of accomplishment.

At times, I felt I would never be able to live through writing this. Looking back always stirs up every part of the memories and makes me think I will surely fall back into the muck for eternity. And yet, I now feel relieved that I have gone through this writing process. The story will now be a part of written history that hopefully helps others.

I have been so blessed to be able to keep my faith in the Triune God. It is so strong, even now. And I believe in my soul that the Catholic Church, the original church ordained by Jesus and started by his hand-picked apostles, is indeed, as the definition of the word catholic states, the Universal Church.

I am even more involved in my parish now than I was in those early years of my life. As I finish this book, I am the Respect Life chairperson, a lector, and a member of the parish council and the women's club. Of course, as a deacon couple, I assist Deacon Steve at baptisms, funeral vigils and funerals. As a couple, we also work with couples in our parish's marriage prep program and the Order of Christian Initiation for Adults.

In the six plus years since Steve's ordination, I have also been able to overcome some things directly connected to Steve's service. I told Steve early on that I would never be able to see him wear a deacon's collar, as it would be too triggering. Through the grace of God, that is no longer a stressor for me, and he wears his collar whenever appropriate. Our God is indeed an awesome God!

I hope this book has given you two things: hope in the almost impossible and love for a good and gracious, ever-present God.

Blessings,
Shannon Shaughnessy Age

Afterword

MOST REVEREND JOSEPH E. KURTZ, DD

Dear Readers,

The past twenty years have produced scores of articles and news headlines about the reality of child abuse and the sins of clergy who have violated their vocation and their call to serve Christ and his Church by such horrendous acts. Few accounts, however, provide such a thorough witness to the reality of what a victim-survivor endures and the great challenges of the path of healing that must follow. In this book, Shannon Age courageously provides an authentic story of pain, hurt and eventual healing. As a survivor of clergy sexual abuse and one who witnessed the same with her sister, Shannon's story is filled with sadness, grief and hurt beyond telling. Uplifting also is her witness to a new dawn through the working of Christ's grace in her life.

During the last fourteen years, I have been privileged to serve as Shannon's Archbishop and have come to treasure the friendship and mutual respect that has developed between Shannon and me. Her journey has been a source of inspiration for me and many others. During this period, Shannon accompanied Steve as he prepared for ordination to the diaconate. Together, they exercised a positive and healthy witness with the other deacon candidates and spouses in supporting a new day for the Catholic Church and our society—a day in which children will live in an environment that is healthy and safe and in which leaders, especially those charged within the Church, will be models of promoting faithfulness to their sacred promises and vows. I salute and thank Shannon Age for her witness to the power of healing in the midst of great pain and suffering.

Most Reverend Joseph E. Kurtz, DD
Archbishop of Louisville

Safety Plan

On September 21, 2009, I made my last suicide attempt.

After my attempt, my therapist and I worked on my personal safety plan. I had never had a plan before then.

So, what is a personal safety plan? It is a specific plan you promise to do when you feel the need to end things. When you make this plan, tell a few people that you absolutely promise to follow this plan. The telling itself makes the promise more real to you and will come back to you, should you ever get in the position of wanting to end your life.

If you are feeling the need to hurt yourself, follow these steps.

First, make sure to get to a safe place away from things you could use to hurt yourself. If you have to, lock yourself in a room away from anything that is dangerous to you and your state of mind.

Next, have a list, perhaps in your phone, of people you can call. It's best if you talk to these people when you make your plan so they know to take your call or text when you are in trouble. You could text something as simple as, "Need help now, not doing well." If the first person you call doesn't answer, you must keep on calling down your list until you make contact with someone. It's imperative that you make contact with someone!

It absolutely does not matter what you physically look like when this happens! You may not have bathed or washed your hair in a week. It doesn't matter! The people on your list would much rather see you dirty and smelly than go to your funeral.

If you go through your list and no one answers, you must call the national suicide hotline at 1-800-273-8255 or simply dial 988. Put that number in your phone too.

God bless you.
You are loved!

Grief to Grace

Grief to Grace has served thousands across the United States and around the world since 2005. The retreat program founded by Theresa Burke, PhD is facilitated by mental health professionals and centered on Jesus Christ's teachings. The Grief to Grace retreats helps those who have endured physical, emotional, sexual and/or spiritual abuse find healing.

Grief to Grace is a five-to-seven-day program. The Living Scriptures, together with journaling, group activities, therapeutic facilitation, cognitive restructuring, discussions and grief work offer an effective healing process grounded in Jesus Christ. It is a pilgrimage to discover the love, tenderness, belonging, safety, joy and peace that are often missing in the experience of abuse victims.

Inspired by the knowledge that wounds can be the vehicle for exploring and revealing the deepest textures of our heart and soul when we journey into the grief, open ourselves safely to the pain, and allow ourselves to be taught, without fear, without holding back, without blame, Grief to Grace supports and assists its participants in this spiritual journey. It helps participants face the depth and tragedy of abuse while reclaiming their value and dignity as daughters and sons of the Living God.

Participants are assured of a safe, confidential environment and a welcoming acceptance by the retreat team. To learn more please go to GrieftoGrace.org.

Ready to Fly?

Shannon Shaughnessy Age knows the importance of sharing one's story to inspire change, empower action and ensure those who feel voiceless know that they don't have to remain that way. There is power in collective conversation and change happens when the darkness is brought into the light.

Shannon is a sought-after speaker as well as writes and facilitates women's retreats. Some of her most requested topics include:

- **We Are Holy**: Women After God's Own Heart
- **Putting the Pieces Back Together**: Women Recovering from Abuse and Violence

Learn more about how you can bring Shannon and her story to your group, organization, church or community by visiting www.Shannon Age.com.

Acknowledgments

Through the years, so many people told me to write this book. I kicked the idea around for over a decade. Always, I was told, this story has to be written.

In 2018, I met my now dear friend, Angie Shaughnessy (no relation). She told me I *must* write the book, but she said she would also help me. Angie brought such a depth of gifts with her, and I finally agreed to put this story to paper.

When I say Angie has gifts, I am being too simple. Angie is a sister of Charity of Nazareth, so she understands the Catholic Church at a depth most can't fathom. Also, before becoming a renowned school principal, she was an English teacher. She has been the first editor of almost every page I have written. As a published author of more than thirty books, Angie knew how to navigate the publishing system. Angie is also a well-known and highly respected attorney who has helped many people, including those who have been abused. When I would hit any snag, she convinced me to push through.

This book would have never been put together as you found it had it not been for the silver hands and tender heart of Stephanie Feger of the emPower PR Group. After getting almost finished with what I thought was a good book, Stephanie asked me to trust her and totally tear it apart and put it back together in a different form. At first, I was crushed to think I would have to redo the whole thing, but Stephanie was right. Her ideas for this book made it so much better. Thank you, love!

I would like to thank Archbishop Emeritus Joseph Kurtz, Dr. Brian Reynolds, and Hans Poppe, JD for their very key additions to the book.

Their perspective is very valuable in showing the breadth and width of this story. They've stood with me and, many times, held me up. I will be forever grateful to all three of you!

Another person who has been absolutely selfless in my journey to write this book is the cover artist, Dr. Rex Lagerstrom. I saw some of Rex's work online and fell in love with it. I contacted Rex, and he agreed to do the cover. After listening to the image I had in my head, and with the help of reading part of the book, Rex was able to create the exact image of a small child coming out of the darkness, with the angel flying with her. His work inspires me to forever keep walking away from the darkness.

Next, I would like to thank the author's portrait photographer, Katie Frazier of Katie Frazier Photography. Katie was able to put at ease a person who hates having her picture made. I would rather have a picture of our pets—Phoenix and Lulu the dogs, and Sassy, the cat—in this book instead of my picture!

Special thanks to my dear friends Carmen Rendon and Stephanie Lawson for their help in getting old documents from the library. Whatever happened to card catalogs in the library?

My high school friend, Kim Katzman, spent many hours on the phone with me, helping me to understand the book-making process. I had never heard the terms book layout and formatting, nor thought of the pictures, letters, and news articles as graphic art. Her years of expertise in graphic design helped me envision in my head what I had to do.

There have been so many friends and family members who have cheered me on and prayed for me in this endeavor. I could not begin to list them all. I would be sorry if I missed anyone, so I will just say thank you, because you know who you are!

My husband, Steve, should get an award for living with me while writing this book. As I am horrible with technology, he found and fixed hundreds of my attempts at putting this story in book form. Ask him sometime how many ways you can lose a document in a computer, and he will probably roll his eyes and tell you he didn't know it was humanly possible to lose as many as I did! And do not tell him he should teach me to copy and paste; he would probably run for the hills.

About the Author

Shannon Shaughnessy Age was born and raised in Louisville, Kentucky, and now lives in a small town outside of Louisville.

She worked professionally as a mammography and radiologic technologist for forty years. She has been a spokesperson and advocate in hunger awareness, clergy sexual abuse, breast cancer awareness and more recently, chairing her church's committee on respecting and aiding those with life issues from conception to natural death. She also enjoys writing retreat plans for topics such as Holy Women of God and Women Recovering from Abuse and Violence.

Shannon and her husband, Steve, are both retired. They enjoy outreach work in their parish and community. They love traveling but also love being home working in their yard. They enjoy spending time with family, friends, Phoenix and Lulu their dogs, and Sassy their cat.

Learn more about Shannon by visiting www.ShannonAge.com.